THE INDIAN THEATRE

THE
INDIAN THEATRE

*A Brief Survey of the
Sanskrit Drama*

BY

E. P. HORRWITZ

Sometime Lecturer in Sanskrit at Trinity College,
Dublin; Assistant Examiner to the Civil
Service Commission

Benjamin Blom
New York

First Published in Glasgow, 1912
Reissued in 1967, by
Benjamin Blom, Inc., New York 10452
Library of Congress Catalog Card No. 67-13329

Printed in U.S.A. by
NOBLE OFFSET PRINTERS, INC.
NEW YORK 3, N. Y.

Preface

The Indian Theatre forms a companion volume to the author's *Short History of Indian Literature* (London, 1907). Supplementary matter dealing with Veda and Vedânta will be published separately, and is to complete the whole.

The Short History has been well received by such eminent authorities as Drs. Deussen and Rhys-Davids. Other distinguished reviewers find fault with the lack of historical sequence. "Das Ganze ist nicht Geschichte, sondern eine gefällig arrangierte Reihe bunter Bilder", is Prof. Oldenberg's opinion. The author laid himself open to the criticism when he yielded to the publisher's wishes, and abandoned, though unwillingly, a more appropriate title. However, as long as the Short History conveys something of the "spirit of Indian literature", love's labour is not lost.

The following pages, in like manner, endeavour to touch the very soul of the old Sanskrit plays. This could not always be done without sacrificing technical details, and making free with the original texts. The dramatic plot is often paraphrased and presented in a modern garb, in order to attract the modern mind.

I have to thank my learned friend, Dr. Louis C. Purser, Public Orator, Dublin University, for reading the proofs and offering valuable suggestions.

Contents

Pronunciation and Spelling

One syllable only is intoned in English words (intelligent), whereas in French and Sanskrit the accent is evenly distributed (intelligent—Himâlaya). The mark over â, î, û in Sanskrit words does not refer to the intonation at all, but indicates the length of the marked vowel in the following manner:—

Sanskrit.		English.	Example.
a	=	mamma [1]	karma
â	=	market	râja
i	=	fit	shiva
final i	=	any	kâli
î	=	feet	sîta
u	=	pull	buddha
final u	=	cuckoo	manu
û	=	pool	sûtra
e	=	day	veda
ai	=	die	adwaita
o	=	no	yoga
au	=	now	bauddha [2]
g	=	go (not gem)	gîta
y	=	yes (not lay)	himâlaya
th	=	ant-hill (not anthem)	atharva

[1] Intoning the first syllable as children do.   [2] i.e. Buddhist.

In order to simplify the spelling, all accents have
been omitted over the final â and î.   Thus Sîtâ and
Kâlî are spelt Sîta and Kâli.[1] Nor have accents been
provided for words sufficiently known in Europe, e.g.
Âryan and brâhmin, Râjput and Kashmîr.   Sikh,
likewise derived from the Sanskrit, sounds like seek.
An English pronunciation should be given to Punjab
and Ganges, also to anglicized terms such as pundit
(scholar) and suttee (burning of widows).[2]

There is a slight difference of sound between sh
in the word nutshell and ch in kitchen.   The latter
is pitched a key higher, being uttered from the palate
or roof of the mouth, while sh is formed in the hol-
lowed tongue.   Both sounds are represented in the
Sanskrit alphabet, but since Kashmir, notwithstand-
ing the palatal sibilant in the Indian script, is the
accepted orthography in England, we have used sh
in transcribing either sound.   The reader will, therefore, find Shiva by the side of Vishnu, although the
god of the Shivaists really bears a palatal initial,
and the name of the rival deity an ordinary sh.

D, n, and t are linguals or tongue sounds in
English, but dentals in Italian.   The countrymen of
Dante pronounce the poet's name by pressing the
tip of their tongue against the teeth.   Sanskrit has
two letters for each of the three consonants, but the
phonetic distinction is hardly noticeable to an Eng-

[1] Latin, too, sacrifices, for the sake of brevity, the vowel length shown
in the final â and î of Indian feminines.   Nova (new) is equal to Sanskrit navâ, and septima (7th) to saptamî.

[2] The Vedic priesthood energetically suppressed compulsory suttee,
a remnant of primeval barbarism, but, like dying embers fanned into
a flame, the hideous custom was subsequently re-established.

lishman. For this reason we transliterate Indian linguals (Vishnu) and dentals (Manu) alike.

Final a and n are occasionally omitted in the modern use of Greek and Latin names, Helen taking the place of Helena, Plato of Platon, and so on. We have followed the classical precedent with regard to several Sånskrit words.

Thus Arjun and Yudhishthir stand for Arjuna and Yudhishthira, râja (king) for râjan, karma (character) for karman. Brahma (God) and âtma (soul) are short for Brahman and âtman; brahmachâri (religious student), sannyâsi (saint), and yogi (devotee) for brahmachârin, sannyâsin, and yogin.

The Platonists of Alexandria looked upon Christ as an emanation of the Godhead, superior in degree, but equal in essence to the rest of mankind. This doctrine they called gnosis, or spiritual cognition, and themselves gnostics, i.e. knowers of the True. In order to call attention to the spiritual kinship which exists between Platonism and Vedânta, the spelling gnâna (self-knowledge) and gnâni (pursuing gnâna) has been adopted in preference to the customary jnâna and jnâni.[1]

---

[1] The above remarks on spelling and pronunciation, together with the footnote on p. 35, as well as the Appendix, are mostly copied, with the publisher's permission, from the author's *Short History of Indian Literature* (T. Fisher Unwin, London).

THE
INDIAN THEATRE

1. In the Court Theatre of Ujain, 1400 years ago

A new play by Kâlidâsa is announced. The first performance is to take place at the Spring Festival, and will be the event of the Ujain season. The citizens are proud of their great poet, and declare with enthusiasm that, in beauty of language and truth of sentiment, no other Indian drama can vie with Shakuntala. It is King Vikrama's gracious pleasure that the play shall be acted at the Royal Castle. The excellent company, the author's high repute, the patronage of the Court, the gladdening springtime, and the elaborate scenic preparations happily combine in a

promise of great success. The splendid
music-room of the castle, generally used
for Court concerts and recitals, has been
made ready for the performance of Shakuntala. The heavy folding-doors, now
replaced by a brocaded stage curtain, lead
to the central court where a large audience
can be accommodated. A circular range
of stately marble columns round which
fresh garlands spirally ascend gives the
open court a classical appearance. Sculp-
tured busts of gods and kings rest, in the
interjacent niches, on massive stands of
blue porphyry, behind splashing cascades
ornamented with quaint shellwork. The
royal tent is pitched in the middle of the
court. Its rich cloth is of Syrian scarlet,
bordered with gold, and lined with pale-
green cashmere. The six posts which
support it are overlaid with beaten silver.
Around their base, and in front of the
stage, is a profusion of choice flowers and
tropical foliage, tastefully arranged in the
national colours of Ujain. The Imperial
standard is waving from a flagstaff erected
by the side of the theatre. The curtain
folds are held together by a handsome
ruby and diamond clasp,—the letters U

and V, initials of the city and the King, being daintily interlaced in the time-hallowed nâgari or urban script.[1] The clasp is to be presented to the poet, for the Râja knows how to honour literary merit.

At last the festive morning dawns. The orchestra plays behind the stage, and, amid the opening bars of the prelude, King Vikrama enters, regally adorned with diadem and purple, and surrounded by his aides-de-camp and high State functionaries. The vassal kings are seated on his right, the Queen and her ladies on the left of the throne. One lady - in - waiting holds a golden lyre and a wreath of immortelles and evergreen, the Queen's souvenir for the laureate. The crimson liveries and peach-coloured waistbands of the black slaves who serve refreshments are pleasantly relieved by the cool-looking lawn

[1] The early Christian communities that sprang up in towns referred to pagan rustics whose huts lay scattered over moor and "heath" as heathens. Gospel truth was slow to permeate the rural districts. Analogously, the Indian peasantry knew neither urbane literature nor the complex Sanskrit type, but town-bred (nâgara) gentlemen were familiar with the nâgari alphabet.—Sanskrit texts which are printed in Western countries dispense, more and more, with the awkward nâgari characters in favour of the simpler Latin script.

dresses, pearl necklaces, and diamond
tiaras of the Court beauties. The palace
court swarms with distinguished guests.
Ministers and savants, brahmins and
kshatriyas, the cream and flower of Ujain
society, are promenading or lounging,
chatting and laughing. Here are some
excited politicians, eagerly discussing the
impending war with some rebellious hill
tribe in Nepal, and there is a group of fine
gentlemen tattling over the latest society
scandal or to-morrow's cock fight. In a
quiet corner the ringing voice of Varâha-
Mihir may be heard; the astronomer-royal
is speaking to a calm-looking, white-
bearded Persian. On the opposite side,
the sparkling eyes and the broad forehead
of Amara Singh are conspicuous. That
famous Court lexicographer, who stoops
slightly, is just handing the final portion
of his Sanskrit Dictionary to a Buddhist
friend, who has come all the way from the
South of China to undertake the translation of the precious manuscript. But now
the gay hum dies away into silence. An
exquisite trio on flute, guitar, and harp is
finished, and youthful choristers, pure-
toned as silver bells, sing praise to the

gods, and greeting to King and clergy.
Then the stage manager comes forward,
pronounces a short benediction, and begs
the illustrious audience in humorous verse
to lend a kindly ear to the entertainment.
The King's chamberlain unclasps the costly
gem, and two figurantes draw aside the
folds of the curtain. Admiring interjec-
tions and the clapping of hands testify that
the beautiful woodland scene with which
the play opens is highly appreciated.
The gurgling of a swollen brook hurrying
down the hillside and wild screams of
waterfowl are heard in the distance. The
golden rays of the morning sun fall through
the branches of some fine old trees upon
the noble features of King Dushyanta.
Dressed in sombre russet, he alights from
his hunting-car, bow in hand, and addresses his charioteer in eloquent Sanskrit
verse. The background of the stage is
raised, and represents a sacred grove with
Kanva's peaceful hermitage. Two nut-
brown maids in rustic garb are watering
the thirsty plants in the tidy garden. The
stage herald, holding a long staff of mi-
mosa wood in his hand, so that he may
conveniently point to the various objects

which he means to explain, now announces
Shakuntala, the heroine of the play. A
thrill of excitement runs through the spell-
bound audience. Will the actress satisfy
or disappoint their high expectations? But
there she comes, clad in a plain frock of
matted bass which veils and yet reveals
her lovely form. The rounded lines of the
girlish face, her large soft eyes and long
downy lashes, the graceful neck and delicate arms, the heaving of her but ill-im-
prisoned bosom, the expressive attitudes
and natural gestures, win every heart.
She opens her lips, and her mouth speaks
music. Vikrama's Court trembles with
delight and deep emotion. Shakuntala,
the latest play by Kâlidâsa, is henceforth
enrolled among the immortal creations of
the world's poetry.

2. The Origin of the Hindu Drama

In the beginning was the Veda, and
divine races peopled the earth. The RIG
VEDA is the oldest portion of Indian
poetry, and the most ancient monument

of Aryan literature. The Rig hymns[1]
extol the grandeur of nature and her
forces, especially Indra the Thunderer,
and Agni, god of fire celestial and terrestrial. The black-skinned aborigines of
the Punjab were as ignorant of Vedic
song and the polished Sanskrit in which
it is embedded as the rude Anglo-Saxons
were of the Chanson de Roland and the
refined Norman tongue. But the churlish
race that sprang from the enslaved Dasyus
grew up in Aryan surroundings, and
learned to speak Sanskrit. Still, they
were excluded from the study of the Rig
Veda, which remained a monopoly of the
higher castes. The privileged classes
alone received Vedic instruction, and, by
virtue of that knowledge, were admitted
to the sacrament of a new birth. None
else was to have the benefit of spiritual
regeneration. But light fell into the darkness, and among the despised shûdras
poets arose who composed out of the
world-old nature lore, magic and exorcism,
another Sanskrit hymnal for the use of the
people. This is the ATHARVA VEDA, which

[1] I.e. hymns of praise, arranged in ten mandalas or cycles of
song.

had to struggle for centuries before the twice-born would reluctantly give it a place in their sacred canon.[1]

While the Rig Veda consists of prayers to the bright elements of nature, the Atharva spells are pervaded by a dread of her dark aspects, and a hankering after occult powers. The Atharva collection, though based on immemorial tradition, is chronologically younger than either the SÂMA VEDA, a book of chants compiled from Rig passages, or the YAJUR VEDA, which contains the Vedic liturgy appointed to be read at sacrificial services.[2]

.   .   .   .

[1] The Laws of Manu do not count the Atharva among the books of the Vedic canon, and the brahmins of the Dekhan reject it even now as apocryphal. The Buddhist Nikâyas ignore the Atharva altogether.

[2] The geographical area of the Rig Veda is confined to the Punjab, and does not yet extend to the Gangetic shores. The Atharva charms represent a stage of culture even older and more primitive, but incantations continued to be added long after the Rig lyrics were complete in that final form which we possess. This accounts for the absence of the king of beasts, most to be dreaded and most powerful, from the Rig fauna, whereas Atharva poetry is familiar with the flecked native of the jungle swamps of Bengal. Subsequently, the tiger's name served as a title of pre-eminence, and the animal's skin became symbolical of royal power. At the coronation ceremony the Râja, clad in a tiger's skin, was enthroned on the "lion-seat". Lion and tiger were looked upon as joint-rulers of the wild life in the forest.

After the creation of the world the golden age commenced. Peace and unity reigned on earth, and all men walked with God. Next came the age of silver, when mankind turned aside from the Divine Will, and everybody followed his own direction. Strife and bloodshed came into existence, but God was merciful, and separated the sexes, creating male and female, that love once more might bind the self-willed race. No sooner did the heart feel drawn to outward things than man lost his power of introspection. The five organs of sense were evolved in order that gods and mortals might quench their thirst for worldly pleasures. Indra, delegated by the other gods, approached the throne of the Godhead, and said: "O Brahma, we wish to feast our eyes and ears on a dramatic spectacle; deign to create the merry play for our enjoyment". And the Creator nodded graciously, and fell into a profound meditation. And out of the Divine Thought sprang the NÂTYA VEDA, that is, the Veda of the Theatre.[1] Such was the Will of the Lord who made

[1] A corruption of nâtya (dancing, acting) or some cognate word is nautch-girl—the name given to a professional dancer in India.

the fifth Veda, drawing the quintessence of the drama out of the four Vedas—dance from the Rig, song from Sâma, mimicry from Yajur, and passion from Atharva. Brahma then summoned Vishwakarma, celestial architect, that he might build a stage in Indra's heaven. The sage Bharata was appointed as theatrical manager and as conductor of the heavenly performances.

Such is the mythical account of the origin of the Indian theatre. In reality, it originated from the ancient custom of reciting the national poetry at social and religious gatherings. The Gangetic tribes were renowned for their gifted bards. The very words bhârata and mâgadha came to mean "minstrel, actor".[1] Bâna, who wrote his famous novel in the age of the Arabian Prophet, relates that the Hindu epics used to be read aloud in various places of worship throughout Kanouj, and that these public recitals were so excellent that royalty often attended. In the rainy season the lecturer's place was at the reading desk in the city temples, but during the fine months of the year the evening entertainment was

[1] Even now actors are called bhats in India, but the name is not directly derived from bhârata.

given on the village green. A fellow-actor expounded the Sanskrit verses to the illiterate villagers in their local patois. The reading of the Mahâ-Bhârata would last several weeks, being continued night after night. So keen was the interest taken in the subject that the dire misfortunes of the Pândava brothers called forth many a sob and tear, whilst their happy return to Hastinapur was hailed with exclamations of joy and sighs of relief, the cottages within earshot being illuminated. When Sanskrit became too choice and high-flown for light street gossip and plain home talk, the prâkrits or vulgar tongues of India pushed themselves more and more to the front. The bhâratas and mâgadhas began to introduce vernacular versions of both epics, and gradually discarded bookish Sanskrit altogether. The interpreter, being needed no longer, henceforth took part in the recitation. Musical accompaniment and dramatic gestures added to the success of the two performers.

The oldest Indian dramas, or rather colloquies (sanvâdas), were not composed in Sanskrit, but in Prâkrit. The Mahâ-Bhârata and Râmâyana supplied no end

of subjects, even as the Bible was the in-
exhaustible source of the mysteries and
miracle plays in medieval Europe. Indeed, originally the Prâkrit sanvâdas were
mysteries too, either Krishna or Shiva
acting and dancing the principal part.
Favourite episodes from the Govinda's
eventful life were the "Slaying of Kansa
the Tyrant" and the "Binding of the
Heaven-storming Titan".[1] Large crowds
came to witness these open-air spectacles.
The grand finale, a merry roundelay of the
bright-eyed Gopis, proved a special attrac-
tion. Rival worshippers flocked in equal
numbers to the wanton bacchanals held
in honour of Shiva. The Vedic priesthood endeavoured to expunge whatever
was lascivious or farcical in the popular
cult of the two primitive gods, but the
sanvâdas, with all their rippling laughter
and gross licence, survived, and were even
cultivated in Sanskrit literature. Some
Vedic hymns have quite a dramatic character.[2] The warfare of the elements is the
ever-recurring theme of the sacred Rig

[1] Bali.

[2] "Les dialogues védiques", says Prof. Sylvain Lévi, to whose
sound scholarship this volume is indebted for much valuable
information, "ne sont ailleurs que des drames rudimentaires."

lyrics, and after once hymning and glori-
fying the striking cosmic phenomena,
what was more natural than to enact the
"divine persons" with dance and song on
high sacrificial feast days? Thundering
Indra and his wild mountain host, the
whistling maruts or storm-gods; irate Agni
leaping forth in the red flash of lightning;
the glistening raindrops trembling with joy
at their release from the burst cloud-castles;
the blushing dawn announcing victorious
Sûrya (the rising sun), and the dancing
sunbeams upholding his gleaming banner
triumphantly—forces of nature, dread or
jubilant, are the dramatis personæ in the
extant sanvâda hymns. But the Vedic
dialogues reflect the afterglow rather than
the first morning flush of the rude representations, staged in the vulgar tongue, of
Krishna's and Shiva's ancient mysteries.
Again, the sublime converse between
Krishna and Arjun, told with consum-
mate art in the Bhagavad Gîta, and the
mystic colloquies held by Shiva and Kâli,
according to the Tantras, are but a late
development of the old Prâkrit sanvâdas
which, even in the age of the Rig Veda,
were no longer fully understood.

Every literary tongue is a stanch conservative, but the people's speech constantly fluctuates and is ever reconstructed. Consequently, writings in dialect are soon antiquated and void of interest save for the philologist, whereas a great national literature outlives the nation. The cherished traditions of the vanished Prâkrit theatre, of which we know nothing but that it must have existed, were silently absorbed by the nascent Sanskrit drama. The earliest Sanskrit plays which are preserved suddenly flash upon our sight like lightning when it breaks through a dark thundercloud. They seem perfect and full-grown as Minerva when she leapt in complete armour from Jove's creative forehead. The countrymen of Homer may well have doubted the miraculous conception of the goddess of wisdom, and questioned her fabled birth without ancestral lineage, but it is quite certain that Kâlidâsa, who generally opens the list of playwrights in native primers of Indian literature, was but the heir and successor of a long line of distinguished Sanskrit dramatists—Saumilla, Bhâsa, and others whom the poet himself acknowledges. These, too, were undoubtedly preceded by reputed writers of Prâkrit plays. This view is corroborated by the existence of an old Sanskrit treatise on dramatic art. The essay, which is ascribed to the sage Bharata, abounds in technical Prâkrit terms, most of them relating to scenic details. Bharata enumerates, at great length, those prâkrits or dialects which, in accordance with established custom, might be used for stage purposes.[1] The subsequent authors of Sanskrit dramas faithfully upheld the theories laid down by Bharata. Indeed, minor rôles were never composed in Sanskrit; the stately tongue would have sounded ludicrous on the homely lips of the vulgar who crowd and enliven the Indian stage. English literature exhibits a similar feature. Guy Mannering, gentleman, does not use sailor slang like Dick Hatteraick, the smuggler, and the provincialisms and grammatical blunders of Adam Bede's old mother widely differ from the cultured and urbane style of the Rev. Mr. Irwine. King Henry the Fifth does not speak broken English like his French lady-love, and Dickens's novels display every shade of metropolitan jargon. In the dramatic literature of India, the

---

[1] The very word nâtya (stage acting) is a Prâkrit term.

prâkrits hold exactly the same position. They appear amidst the glossy Sanskrit dialogue like a shabby camel driver among the rich and elegant court dresses of a native durbar. The part of the vidûshaka or jester is written, as a rule, in a dialect of the eastern provinces. Scoundrels are made to talk Ujain slang, and intriguers a patois of the Dekhan. Shâkâri, another corrupt dialect, seems to be ultimately derived from the Shakas or steppe riders who invaded India at various times. Here they learned to speak Prâkrit, but peculiarities of speech such as the sound given to sibilants showed their foreign nationality, just as the pronunciation of *r* or *th*, if nothing else, betrays a French or German resident in England. Soldiers and salesmen, publicans and pastrycooks, and the many other trades and professions introduced in the Indian theatre, all speak a prâkrit of their own, varying but slightly from one another. Gods and brahmins, kings and nobles, converse in faultless Sanskrit, but women speak Prâkrit. In one play, a celestial congratulates Shiva and Uma on the occasion of their marriage; the bride is addressed in Prâkrit, the bridegroom in Sanskrit.

The Agra district is the holy land of Krishnaism. Shauraseni, the medieval speech of the Agra populace, is frequently met with in Sanskrit plays. The Krishna cult has been successfully revived in Bengal, and numerous yâtras or melodramas have been composed in honour of the god. Yâtras are very popular in the Presidency, and preserve the Shauraseni dialect, which has long changed from a vulgar to a sacred tongue.[1]

Bharata, who has become the tutelary deity of the Indian theatre, is not a his-

[1] The gentle art of poetry was cultivated at Magadha, and after the rise of the Guptas, at the Courts of Kanouj and Berar. Mâgadhi and Shauraseni, the two leading Prâkrits, originated, the one in Oudh, and the other west of Kanouj. Queen Damayanti, who knew the magic of soul-stirring song, was a native of Vidarbha, as Berar was then called because of its "grassless" plains. At one time, the mahâ-râshtra or "great kingdom" of Berar extended from the Vindhya slopes to the river Krishna, and touched the western and the eastern seas. The diction of the Vidarbha poets became a standard of literary grace and simplicity. Under their refining influence, the Magadha patois that prevailed at Berar was moulded into Mahârâshtri, which Dandin, a Kanouj romancer of the seventh century A.D., exalts above all other prâkrits. Mahârâshtri, after giving birth to Marathi, the language of the Mahrattas, shared the fate of Pâli, and became a priestly tongue. The sacred writings of the Jains, a brother-sect of the Buddhists, with whom they hold many doctrines in common, are partly composed in Mahârâshtri. The relation of Prâkrit and Pâli to Sanskrit is fully discussed in the *Short History of Indian Literature*, chapter xix.

torical person, but a symbolic name like Vyâsa or Manu. The treatise which goes by his name is very prolix, and may be an amplification of the Bhârata Sûtras which are lost. It is to these sûtras, or stage directions for the use of bhâratas or actors, that Bharata owes his imaginary existence. They were written in Sanskrit, but their ultimate source was obviously some Prâkrit dramaturgy. The sûtras must be very old, since they were studied at the Universities of Hindustan before the Macedonian regiments set foot on Indian soil. The Bhârata Sûtras are mentioned by Pânini, the greatest of Indian grammarians, who is generally referred to the fourth century B.C.[1] The aphorisms were still extant at the time of Alfred, King of England, when Shivaswâmi, an Indian wit, rudely compared their obscure style to the dark waters of the Jumna. As Christian principle rests on the precepts of the Church, and as English law is administered in agreement with precedent, so the Sanskrit theatre has conformed to the rules laid down in the

[1] In the history of linguistic science, Pânini's elaborate Sanskrit Grammar is as epoch-making as the masterpieces of Grimm, Zeuss, Diez in the cognate fields of Teutonic, Celtic, and Romance philology.

Bhârata Sûtras.   They were held almost
sacred by Kâlidâsa and other dramatists.
What wonder then that a myth arose de-
claring that the sage Bharata had copied
them from the fifth Veda, which was believed to be a creation of Brahma himself.

3. An Indian Love Story

On the wings of song I carry my beloved to the fairy banks
of the Ganges (Heine).[1]

In the days gone by when celestial
nymphs did not disdain to descend on
earth, and bestow their affections on mortal
kings and heroes, and when the gods made
known their will through the mouths of
seers and prophets, there lived in the
north of India a royal sage, King Vishwâmitra, who had renounced the glories of
dominion and the pleasures of earth, to
attain the more lasting joys of heaven.
So austere were his devotions, and so
rigid his penances, that nature could no
longer withhold her secrets from him, and
he was able to direct her occult forces.

[1] Auf Flügeln des Gesanges,
   Herzliebchen, trag ich dich fort,
   Fort nach den Ufern des Ganges:
   Dort weisz ich den schönsten Ort.

The heavenly host became jealous of the saint's increasing power, and they called on Indra, the supreme god, and said: "Frustrate, O mighty one, the full fruition of Vishwâmitra's piety, otherwise he might endanger even your well-established position". And Indra gravely listened to the representations of the sub-gods, and feeling uneasy lest St. Vishwâmitra should really overthrow him, and take his place in heaven, he bade Menaka, a beautiful fairy, go down to the shores of the river Gautami, where the yogi sat near the roots of venerable trees, his passions subdued, and his mind withdrawn from the world, and by her youthful charms disturb the profound meditation of the self-centred sage. Menaka, by the skill of her sex, succeeded only too well with Vishwâmitra. Desire arose in him, and from his and the nymph's embraces a baby-girl was born, destined to be the tribal mother of powerful nations in the time to come.

After the birth of the child, Menaka, by the will of Indra, reascended to heaven, and left the babe embedded in soft green moss, the cloudless Indian skies smiling on her through the waving leafage over-

head, and gentle breezes kissing her to
sleep, while the running brook by her side
murmured a sweet lullaby. But Vishwâmitra felt humiliated that the gods had
foiled his aspirations, and that he had
allowed himself to yield to the allurements
of a nymph. In his shame and resentment, he left the Gautami valley, and
walked towards the setting sun into the
wilds and solitude of the Punjab forests,
vowing under no consideration to be drawn
back to the household life, but to live
alone in holy communion with his great
soul, far away from the haunts of men,
in congenial seclusion. And at last silence
fell on his troubled breast, and he heard
a voice saying: "Of your vow I approve,
my son, but not of the disregard for your
child." And lo! a flock of shakunta birds
suddenly darkened the horizon, and flut-
tered about the sage as if to remind him
of his fatherly duties; and he, the illumined
one, understood. Yet, unwilling to break
his pledge, and be bound by family ties,
Vishwâmitra breathed a holy mantra, to
the effect that the little one should be
taken care of, and his thoughts took
wing, and reached the devout heart of

St. Kanva, sweet singer of the Rig Veda.
And Kanva, in eager response to the master's message, set out from his âshram,
which lay in lonely woods on the southern
slopes of snow-capped Himalay; and
while the rishi proceeded along the flower-
tufted banks of the foaming mountain
stream, large-feathered shakuntas flew
before him, and guided his steps to the
woodland glen where, in a mossy couch,
the tender-limbed babe peacefully slum-
bered. And St. Kanva took the child up
in his arms, and christened her Shakuntala, because kindly shakunta birds had
watched over her, and protected her against
the dangers of the forest. And Shakuntala grew up in St. Kanva's hermitage under
her foster-father's loving care and attention.

Now, the grove where the âshram or
hermitage was situated formed part of a
large kingdom which, in a later age, was
peopled by the powerful Bhârata tribe.
But long before the Bhâratas waged their
fierce wars in the fertile valley of the
Upper Ganges, a renowned King, Dushyanta by name, reigned over their grand-
sires, and held his illustrious Court in the
wealthy city of Hastinapur, not far from

the site of modern Delhi.[1] Dauntless in battle was Dushyanta, and prudent in council; a fine type of the Heroic Age which the Mahâ - Bhârata epic like a gigantic painting unfolds, in gorgeous colours, before our wondering gaze. After attending to the endless petitions and grievances of his subjects, day after day, the conscientious Monarch would gladly relieve the pressure of public business by a week's sport in the richly-stocked woods of his northern provinces. There at least he could forget for a time all state affairs, and delight once more in chasing the foam-flecked buffalo and the black-eyed antelope. One day, when the royal hunts-man hotly pursued a swift-footed fawn·

[1] Vishwâmitra himself had been the gallant leader of that martial clan. An exquisite folk-ballad, composed in the san-vâda style (Rig Veda III, 33) extols the heroic warrior-saint who led the proud Bhârata host across the rapid currents of the Punjab streams forth into battle.

The suffix in Hastina-pur recurs in metro-pol-is (mother-city). Greek *pol* and Sanskrit *pur* signify the *full* or po-pul-ous "town" contrasted with the deserted jungle. Like a typical Aryan, the monosyllable has travelled extensively. It can be traced from Singa*pore* to Sebasto*pol*, and from Constantino*ple* to Na*ples*, and Greno*ble* in the Alps. Cities of hunters and elephants are implied in the names of Shikar*pur* on the Indus, and Hastina*pur* near Delhi. India, north of the river Krishna, teems with purs or ancient boroughs. Udaipur, Jodhpur, and Jaipur are all in Rajputana.

across the "merry greensward", the terrified deer fled into a sacred grove, as
though it expected shelter from the saintly
inhabitants, and protection against the
deadly arrows of the cruel sportsman.
And, indeed, its looks of agony and dumb
prayer were not left unanswered, for out
of a forest hut came a holy anchorite, and
raising his hands he addressed Dushyanta:

"Mighty Sovereign, slay not the help-
less creature! The weapons of virtuous
kings and warriors should be used for the
relief of the oppressed, and not for the
destruction of the innocent."

The appeal to virtue and kingly duty
was not made in vain to the noble Dushyanta; and humbly saluting the pious re-
cluse, the Monarch dropped his richly-
ornamented bow, and begged permission to
enter St. Kanva's hermitage, and pay homage to the holy preceptor. That was readily
granted, and descending from his hunting-
car, the King thus spoke to his charioteer:

"That we stand on consecrated ground
we cannot doubt. Hallowed grains lie
scattered beneath the aged trees, so that
the green-breasted parrot-mothers in yon
pendent nests may feed their unfledged

young. Confident are the shy gazelles, not startled at the sound of human voices as in the public parks of Hastinapur. You see the one over there? Look how it skips about with long steps, while others nibble the soft cool grass, now and then pausing with their mouths half open. Tops of kusha grass have been cut for some religious rite, and are sprinkled about. The glaze on these fresh leaves is dull, owing to the smoke which rises from a sacrificial oblation of barley and clarified butter. The young roebucks, without fear at our approach, quietly graze on the pleasant lawn which slopes down to the riverside. But groves devoted to religion should be entered in humbler garments."

And Dushyanta, ever considerate of other people's feelings, took off his jewel-studded hunting-coat, and left it, together with all regal ornaments, in charge of his faithful charioteer, whom he bade return to the forest glade, where the royal tent and pavilion had been pitched. And in the simple wayfarer who now approached the âshram none could recognize royalty any longer. St. Kanva happened to be absent on a pilgrimage, and Dushyanta, attracted

by the beautiful scenery around him,
begged leave to enter the garden of the
hermitage, then bright with gay flowers
and the promise of luscious fruit. A
well-kept path led him to a natural bower
of jasmine bushes, prettily embellished
with large fragments of rough stone. It
was indeed a lovely spot, which fairies and
genii might have chosen for sport and
frolic in a fine midsummer night. The
golden sunbeams, from a canopy of purple
clouds, streamed through the fragrant
morning air upon the pearl-dewed mea-
dows. In the distance the river Malini
was winding its graceful course; some
amorous flamingos stood on the pebbly
bank partly hidden by overhanging
branches. Beyond, a grassy plain with
browsing chamara herds; and far away
a lofty range of hills, bathed in a flood of
light, and encircled by flights of blue-
necked pigeons. Dushyanta's enchanted
eye rapidly passed along the Alpine ridges
which gradually died away in the majestic
peaks of mist-enwrapped Himâlaya,

" where musky breezes throw
Their balmy odours o'er eternal snow".[1]

[1] Wintry *Him*alay is connected with Latin *hiems* (winter).

And the King's vision slowly travelled
back again to his nearer surroundings.
Almost in front of him there grew a
spreading mango tree, a couple of sleepy
antelopes crouching in its shade, and
mantles of woven bast suspended on its
branches, to be dried by the kindly sunbeams. And round the thick stem of the
tree a slender creeper twined, in full bloom
just then. And in the bloom of youth was
the maiden who stood admiring in front of
the creeper. Beauty flowed in every movement of her graceful limbs. Sweet-smell-
ing shirîsha blossoms hung behind her
delicate ear, the tender filaments waving
over her health-glowing cheek. Her wrists
were adorned with bracelets made of wild
flowers, and she looked like a flower herself, pure and fresh as breath of morning
on the pine-clad hills. When Dushyanta
beheld her—O miracle of the human heart!
—the fair landscape before him lost all its
charm, and faded away; and while golden
fancies filled his heart, the musical cadence
of a girlish voice fell on his ear:

" Do you know, my Anasûya, why Shakuntala gazes on that creeper with such
intense delight?"

And the smiling answer came back:
"No, indeed, my Priyamvada! unless
her eyes are spell-bound, and her ears are
charmed with the native music of the
mango tree."

"In summer it is pleasant to hear,
  In autumn it rustles all withered and sear,
  It moans and whistles through the winter drear."

Priyamvada, her bright eyes dancing with
merriment, retorted:
"Oh no! that's not what darling Shakuntala has on her mind. 'As the tender
creeper has chosen the noble mango for a
bridegroom, and lovingly clings to him,
thus do I hope to be united to a noble
husband one day.' That's what she longs
for in her secret heart. Have I not guessed
aright, my Shakuntala?"

But Shakuntala, her young face suffused
with blushes, said evasively:
"I really must go and water the droop-
ing jasmine, or the blossoms will languish
for want of moisture."

So she ran to the fragrant bushes, shame-
faced and looking on the ground; and
when she raised her soft gazelle eyes, they
met Dushyanta's noble face. And hark!

the heart-born god, shaper of form and beauty here below, God Kâma, who ever takes delight in giving pain to lovers, has already strung his flower-wreathed bow, and his never-failing arrow, tipped with the golden flames of love, whizzes along the perfumed breeze, and strikes the heart of fair Shakuntala, the maiden-conqueror of the hero-king whom none could conquer on the battlefield.[1]

Dushyanta greeted her with courteous ease—"May your devotion prosper, holy maid!" And she, in sweet confusion, returned the greeting; but Priyamvada, more self-possessed and ever dignified of speech, on observing a stranger, walked up to him, and bade him welcome in the âshrama.

"Go to the cottage, my Shakuntala!" she said, "and fill a basket with ripe mangoes and rose-apples. Our visitor stands in need of some refreshment, and we must be hospitable, and show due honour to a guest."

Dushyanta begged them not to take any trouble on his account. "Lady, I am not hungry, and your pleasing words are sufficient honour unto me."

[1] God Kâma, the flower-winged archer-boy, is the Hindu Cupid.

Anasûya asked him to be seated, as he must be fatigued after his long journey. "For your accent tells me that you were bred and born far from these rustic parts." And the King, in acknowledging her courtesy, expressed his pleasure at being in such a beautiful place.

"The air is delightful here," he said. "How refreshing is the cool wind which gently moves the bending water lilies in yon pond, and wafts sweet odours from all sides!"

Then they all sat down, and Anasûya enquired:

"Gentle stranger, your refined speech encourages me to ask a question. To what illustrious family do you belong? where is your native country, and who are your noble kinsmen? They must be sorely grieved at your absence. Pray, tell us, what induced you to enter these remote woods, only inhabited by simple anchorites?"

The King, not wishing to make himself known yet, slowly replied:

"Excellent maid, I am a student of the Veda, and dwell in the city of King Dushyanta. Desirous to discharge the religious duties which our Holy Scriptures enjoin, I have come to this sacred grove, because it is reported to be the sanctuary of all virtues."

"Then be welcome again and again!" exclaimed Anasûya, joyfully, "for you are engaged in the same holy labour as our venerable father Kanva. O that he were here just now, and could converse with you!"

"Indeed, you express my heart's desire," rejoined Dushyanta. Then Anasûya was called away to do some household work, and Priyamvada was busy in the garden. Again, Shakuntala was left alone with the King, and their tremulous voices blended in harmony, and their hearts drew nearer in sweet fellowship, and soul rushed into soul until both were like one. And Shakuntala told her lover the simple story of her uneventful life, and time flew like a dream on the golden wings of love. When Shakuntala spoke of her father, Vishwâmitra, once a mighty ruler in Hindustan, Dushyanta, in order to test her, observed that a poor brahminical student was hardly justified in aspiring to the hand of a king's daughter. Shakuntala wept a little as she made reply:

"As my noble father has renounced kingship for higher, holier things, so I gladly renounce my title to royal descent, if need there be, for thy affection, O thou of priestly caste."

Dushyanta, satisfied with this test of her love, then made himself known to be King in the land, and asked Shakuntala to be his Queen. And as in spring, after soft showers, the pearly drops hanging on bush and tree sparkle like diamonds in the sun, so shining tears still glistened on Shakuntala's radiant face, when Dushyanta put on her finger his signet-ring on which the royal name was engraved.

Priyamvada, divining what had happened, called Anasûya from the cottage, but in the midst of their congratulations and rejoicings a royal courier arrived from Hastinapur in search of the King, whom he had traced to the âshram by the help of the charioteer. The messenger brought grave political despatches which necessitated the Monarch's immediate return to the capital. As it was uncertain how long Dushyanta would be absent on the military campaign which he anticipated, it was agreed between the betrothed to solemnize their nuptials at once. The King promised to send a befitting suite of high-born officers and noble matrons, to conduct Queen Shakuntala from the hermitage to the palace, with all honours due to her exalted station. On the evening of the following day, the reluctant Monarch was obliged to leave.

After his departure, the young wife was often seen musing in the jasmine bower where she had first met her lover. Now, one day, a religious mendicant passed St. Kanva's hermitage, and seeing Shakuntala, asked her for a morsel of food and a cup of water, but she, intent on nothing but her absent lord, did not heed the request. Then the old man's wrath blazed up, being kindled by what seemed to him intentional neglect, and evil-boding were the words he spoke:

"As you are so utterly regardless of holy friars' needs, even so shall he, on whom your present thoughts are fixed, fail to remember you when as a humble petitioner you approach him."

Shakuntala's fancy was too fully pre-occupied with anxious thoughts about Dushyanta to be even conscious of the ill-wishes which her absent-mindedness had drawn on her. But Anasûya had been an involuntary witness of the painful scene. In her excitement and sorrow, she ran up to the friar, and, falling at his feet, tried to appease him:

"Holy man, forgive, I entreat you, the offence of an amiable girl who has the highest veneration for you, but, distracted by an excess of love, she did not even know that you spoke to her."

The gentle appeal had the desired effect, and softened the proud heart to which it was addressed.

"Maiden," returned the mendicant, "my words cannot be recalled, but the spell which they have raised shall be broken, and the King's failing memory be restored the moment he sees the ring which Shakuntala has received from him."

The mysterious stranger then disappeared, and Anasûya, to spare the feelings of Shakuntala, resolved for the present to conceal from her what had occurred.

And the days rolled on, and the weeks passed by, but no news came from Dushyanta. Shakuntala often looked pensive and sad, but never harboured any misgivings as to his faithfulness. "She touched her lute, and petted her birds, and slowly counted, amid tears and deep-drawn sighs, the long and weary hours that used to be like minutes." Her own faith was so strong and pure that she could not disbelieve in him.

> "Trusting as the moments fly,
> Trusting as the days go by!"

Yes, trust she would. But why had he not sent the promised escort? No ill could have befallen the great King without her hearing of it. Ah, perhaps he did not like her to arrive at Court during his absence, but rather meant her to stay at home until his return from the campaign. Yes, it must be that; it was all done out of consideration for her comfort. Poor Shakuntala! She was quite unaware of the potent spell and its evil effect on her husband, who had long returned to Hastinapur. But his memory was impaired, his conjugal affection destroyed, and he had lost all recollection of his wedded wife.

And the seasons followed each other in due succession, until genial spring clad hill and dale once more in festive garb. Shakuntala waited and trusted still. She felt somewhat troubled at her husband's prolonged absence, and at the thought that her foster-father might disapprove of her secret marriage. St. Kanva had only just come home from the long pilgrimage which he had undertaken, and celebrated his safe return by a sacrifice to the gods. And as he worshipped before the consecrated hearth where the sacramental fire was blazing, and chanted holy Vedic hymns, a voice spake from out the sacred flame:

"Know, pious brahmin, that your adopted child has received from Dushyanta a ray of glory destined to rule the world even as the sacrificial wood becomes impregnated with mystic fire."

St. Kanva then knew, and seeing Shakuntala embraced her tenderly.

"Sweet child, be comforted. I know about your marriage, and give my consent with all my heart. May the son to whom you will give birth, bright as the rising day star, become a wise and beneficent ruler of India! But it is in accordance with the precepts of our holy religion that a

Prince should be born in his father's house,
and so I have decided to send you to the
palace of your rightful lord. Be ready by
to-morrow morning, beloved child. The
matron Gautami and our pious brother
Shârngarava shall accompany you to
Hastinapur. Dry your tears, my Shakuntala! I, too, am grieved that we must
part. Think of all the joy and love which
await you in your new home, and which
you so well deserve, dear child!"

Next day, at sunrise, Shakuntala uplifted her beaming face to the golden
dawn, and prayed:

"O brilliant goddess, whose daily
awakening sheds gladness over everything, let me adore thy divine splendour
which once more has chased away the
shadows of the dark-winged night. O
radiant dawn, dispel all darkness and distrust from my frail heart; and as trees and
blossoms, in this gladsome springtime,
shine brighter in thy roseate light, grant,
mighty goddess, that I, thy humble devotee, and the unborn child may find
favour in King Dushyanta's sight."

She had not gone far from the cottage
when she met Anasûya, who brought gar-

lands of young leaves and flowers to adorn her friend with these simple tokens of her love, on the last morning which Shakuntala spent at her forest home.

"A Queen deserves far richer apparel," began Anasûya, "than these rude flowers; but they are the gayest ornaments I could find in the woods."

While the two friends caress and kiss each other, the rustling breeze softly whispers to the tree-tops, until the wood nymphs who abide in them shake their leafy crowns, and shower lavish gifts at the Queen's feet. There is a dainty wedding gown, glittering as though woven with pale moonbeams and twinkling stars, and jewels worthy of a Queen are sparkling on the emerald green like dewdrops when they catch the first beam of the morning sun.

Just then St. Kanva came up. He gave his blessing to Shakuntala, and praised her goodness before all the forest:

"O ye green things of the earth, and ye forest trees, to-day our Shakuntala is going to the palace of her chosen lord. She who gave you water first before she drank of it, and out of love for you plucked not

one of your tender leaves, though she
would have liked to decorate with them
her flowing tresses; she whose chief delight
was in the season of spring, when your
branches, ye trees of the grove, are be-
spangled with young blossoms."

And hark! a tuneful response from invisible fairies was wafted through the scent-
laden air:

"May the Queen's path be attended
with prosperity! May propitious breezes
scatter the fragrant dust of gay blossoms
for her delight! May brooks of clear
water, verdant with lotus leaves, refresh
her as she journeys! And may shady
branches be her defence against the
scorching sunbeams!"

And the glad music filled Shakuntala's
soul with joy, and, walking round the
trees, she blushed and smiled as she bowed
to the unseen nymphs.

Meanwhile her travelling companions
and Priyamvada had arrived, the hour of
parting being near at hand. All living
things in the grove seemed to bemoan
Shakuntala's departure. No longer fed
the wistful gazelles on the delicious grass;
the peahens had stopped their coquettish

dance on the lawn; the very plants had lost their strength, and dropped pale leaves. The Queen, seeing her favourite mâdhavi plant covered with beautiful pink blossoms, exclaimed:

"Most radiant of twining plants, let me embrace thee for a last time, and thou return my caresses with thy pliant arms! Though removed far away, I shall always remember thee, sweet plant; but now I must leave thee to the care of my two friends."

Priyamvada and Anasûya sobbed aloud:

"Alas! dearest Shakuntala, when you are gone, in whose care shall we be left?"

But Kanva gently rebuked them:

"Our Shakuntala ought rather to be strengthened by your cheerfulness than depressed by your tears."

And so the little group moved on until they came to the end of the grove,—about a day's journey from the caravan road which led to Hastinapur. Suddenly Shakuntala called out with a start:

"What's that clinging to my skirt, and holding me back? Do look, Anasûya!"

And lo! there was a little fawn, looking up with gently pleading eyes, and unwilling to leave his protectress who had so often fed him with a handful of grains, and smeared his bleeding mouth with healing oil when the sharp blades of grass had wounded it.

"Tender fawn," cried Shakuntala, "why do you look so distressed now that I am about to leave our common home? As I reared you when you had lost your mother, who died soon after your birth, so will my foster-sisters look after you when we two are separated. Go back, my pet, go back, for we must part."

Shârngarava now reminded her not to tarry any longer.

"The sun has risen to a considerable height; let the Queen hasten her departure!"

And turning to his teacher, he enquired:

"Holy sage, be pleased to tell me how I am to address the King when I present Shakuntala to him."

St. Kanva remained silent, but Anasûya observed:

"Look at this water-bird, my Shakuntala. His mate is almost hidden by white lotuses, but you can hear her shrill cries. Yet he disregards her call, and, dropping from his yellow beak long fibres of juicy stalks, gazes at you affectionately. How sad it must be to be neglected by those nearest and dearest to us! My friend, should the virtuous monarch not recollect you at once, promise me to show him your engagement ring."

Shakuntala turned deadly pale, and said:

"What do you mean, my Anasûya? My heart flutters at the mere thought of your cruel suggestion."

And her tears flowed fast. But Priyamvada, ever discreet and gentle, spoke soothing words:

"Weep not, my sister. Love often raises spectres of woe which are dispelled by reality as bad dreams by the morning light."

St. Kanva now raised his voice:

"My son Shârngarava, remember, when you present Shakuntala to the King, to address him in this manner: 'Most gracious Sovereign, we who dwell in holy âshrams are poor in gifts, but rich in devotion. O King, this is Kanva's message to thee: The contract of marriage, reciprocally made between thee and my daughter, I confirm with sincere regard.

Since thou art known to be the most
honourable of men, and my Shakuntala
is the image of virtue, your union will
prove a happy one. Receive her then out
of my hands, great King, and may she
always be honoured by thee and looked
upon with tender affection.'"

"My child," proceeded the sage, "when
you are settled in the palace of your husband, show becoming reverence to him,
and to those whom he reveres. In your
conduct to the domestics be kindly, never
proud, and always just. On no occasion
seek eagerly for your own gratification.
By such behaviour a young wife gains
respect. And now, my well-beloved, give
me and your two sisters a parting embrace."

Shakuntala, a big tear lurking under her
silken eyelashes, pleaded:

"Dear father, must Anasûya and Priyamvada return to the hermitage?"

"Yes," answered the old man; "they
too must be suitably married, and it would
not be proper for them to visit the city."

Once more they all embraced before they
parted.

Shakuntala was just about to disappear

behind the forest trees when St. Kanva waved his hand, and called out after her:

"Shivena gamyatâm, Shakuntale, gamyatâm shivena!" ("May your journey be auspicious, my Shakuntala, an auspicious journey!")[1]

The sage then turned back, and, holding one hand over his eyes,—

"Ah me!" he thought, "my unstable mind has again attained its due balance after the departure of my Shakuntala. In truth, a daughter must sooner or later be the property of another man, and having now sent her to her rightful lord, I feel relieved and tranquil again, like a trustee who has returned a precious deposit of which he had charge to the legitimate owner."

4. The Fatal Ring

When Dushyanta was informed that a brahmin had arrived at his capital from the northern provinces with a message from a saint, the pious King at once sent

---

[1] The flashing stormcloud which purifies the air is called shiva (auspicious) in the Rig Veda, and was subsequently chosen by the brahmins as a symbol for the Deity who destroys the impure and ungodly. Shivena means "with Shiva; with God's blessing". Gamyatâm = may you go.

one of his noblest officers to conduct the holy man to the palace, and receive him with all honours due to the priestly caste. Shârngarava, closely followed by Gautami and Shakuntala, was ushered into the royal presence. Dushyanta was busy meting out judgment and equity alike to the rich and poor, and the young brahmin exclaimed enthusiastically:

"It is ever thus! fertile trees are bent by an abundance of fruit, clouds are brought low when they teem with salubrious rain, and the real benefactors of mankind are neither elated by riches nor puffed up by success. Sire, may victory always attend thy flag, and may the gods bless our beloved Sovereign!"

To the King's gracious enquiry if St. Kanva prospered, and what his announced message conveyed, the self-confident answer was given:

"Great Monarch, descendant of a hundred Kings! they who gather the fruits of devotion may command prosperity. My venerable teacher salutes thee, O Mahâ-Râja, and enquires whether the royal arms are successful. This is his message: 'Illustrious King! the contract of marriage made

between thee and this my daughter I confirm with sincere regard. And since thou
art known to be the most honourable of
men, and my Shakuntala is the image of
virtue, your union will prove a happy
one. Receive her then out of my hands
as thy lawful wife; and may she always
be honoured by thee, Sir King, and looked
upon with tender affection.' "

Shakuntala, her large lotus eyes bent on
the ground, felt her heart throb violently—
"O my heart, why dost thou palpitate?
Remember thy lord's affection, and be
calm!"

While Shârngarava was speaking, an expression of the utmost amazement passed
over the King's features. And with a touch
of scorn he replied:

"What do you say, Sir Monk? that I
am the lady's husband? You seem to have
an inventive turn of mind."

Shakuntala almost fainted with anguish,
and heaved a sigh—"O my heart, thy fears
have proved just!"

But Shârngarava retorted with indig-
nation:

"Does it become a powerful Monarch
to deviate from the path of religion and

honour, merely because he repents of his engagements? Indeed, earthly power and greatness seem to intoxicate the mind, and render even great Kings fickle and arbitrary."

The virtuous Dushyanta did not resent the rude speech, but rejoined calmly:

"I have no knowledge of this lady, far less of my alleged marriage to her. How then can I lay aside all consideration for my military caste, and admit to my palace a young woman who obviously belongs to another husband?"

"Ah me," cried Shakuntala, "the tree of my hopes, which had risen so luxuriantly, is broken down all at once. O my husband, do you not know me any longer?"

Her tears flowed copiously, and she leaned for support on Gautami.

"It is evident," returned Dushyanta with bitterness, "that this beautiful woman has been instructed, for some base purpose, to vilify my name, and drag me down from the dignity which I have hitherto supported. Thus does a stream which has burst its banks, and changed its placid course, uproot the noble trees which grow aloft by the riverside."

"If he has no longer any affection for me," thought Shakuntala, almost bereft of hope, "what is the good of recalling the past with all its sacred joys of love? Yet I will try!" and gathering up fresh courage, she addressed Dushyanta, the colour mounting to her pallid cheeks:

"O my husband! or if the just application of this holy word be still doubted by you—my King! if you have said all this from mere want of recollection, let me restore the King's memory by showing him a gem which, on a happier day, his lavish hand bestowed on me. But oh! where is my ring? Ah, I unhappy woman, I have lost it."

"Poor child," said Gautami, weeping herself, "the ring must have dropped from your finger when you washed your face in the Sachitîrtha pond where we rested yesterday."

Dushyanta shook his head disdainfully, but Shakuntala, in an agony of despair, roused herself to a last effort, and exclaimed:

"O thou of Puru's race, King Dushyanta, I will remind you of another incident. Do you not remember the day when we sat in the fragrant jasmine bower, and you poured water into your hollow hand out of a cup-shaped lotus leaf? A little fawn which I had reared came near, and you said kindly: 'Gentle fawn, drink first.' But he would not drink out of a stranger's hand, yet took the water eagerly from mine, and you said with increasing tenderness: 'Indeed, all creatures love their likes. You, my Shakuntala, and the soft-eyed fawn are both children of the forest; both equally simple and sweet.'"

"Oh, do not let me hear any more of these honeyed falsehoods," cried Dushyanta impatiently.

Thus publicly insulted and disgraced, Shakuntala drew herself proudly up, and spoke with scorn-flashing eyes and passion-raised voice:

"O void of honour, you measure every-one by your bad heart. Was ever Prince like you that wears the bright garb of virtue and religion, but in truth is a base deceiver, treacherous like a deep well whose mouth is overgrown with smiling plants?"

Icy, but free from malice, came back the King's reply:

"The heart of Dushyanta, young woman, is known to all, but your own heart is betrayed by your present bad behaviour."

Shakuntala covered her face, and sobbed like a little child. Shârngarava, whose eyes were fixed on the King, could hardly suppress his righteous anger.

"O Mahâ-Râja," he said at last with forced calmness, "we have obeyed the commands of our holy preceptor, and now beg leave to retire. Shakuntala is your wife by law, no matter if you acknowledge or desert her. Come, sister Gautami, let us depart."

The two left the Council Chamber. Shakuntala bemoaned her adverse fortune, and prayed to the gods that she might be taken to some retreat where none would stand between her shame and conscience. And Menaka, her mother in Indra's heaven, took pity on her unhappy child. Dressed in white robes of light, the nymph descended from her bright abode, and raising Shakuntala above the dark earth, guided her into the realms of peace.[1]

---

[1] Mephistopheles has been allegorically interpreted as Faust's rebellious intellect, and Shakuntala as Dushyanta's neglected

.   .   .   .

Several years had passed, when one day
a poor fisherman who plied his scanty
trade in the lake district of Sachitîrtha
caught a large carp, and upon opening the
fish discovered a costly ring in it. The
old man went up to Hastinapur, and

soul. Sanskrit poets, who, like the rest of their Indian countrymen, firmly believe in transmigration, compare the "migrating
soul" to a migratory shakunta. The word may be a redupli-
cative noun like cock or cuckoo, and would then be literally the
Greek kyknos, our cygnet. Another bird of passage, the
milk-white hansa, has become the Hindu emblem of undying
love, which, out of its native heaven, flutters but timidly in the
dull cage of flesh. A flame-beaked hansa disclosed King
Nala's worth and yearning to the "soul-disturbing" (chitta-
pramâthin) royal maid of Vidarbha.

"To Vidarbha's stately city flew the wild swans tinged
        with gold",

narrates the Mahâ-Bhârata.

The poet-symbolists of Egypt and Greece painted boundless
love as a purple-hued phœnix. The sacred bird is consumed
to ashes by his flaming heart, but on love's wings rises trans-
figured from the pyre.

The pagan Teutons, too, chose the wild swan as a symbol
of the coy soul which shrinks from scoffers and sceptics. The
soul is a ray of eternal light, and reveals her hidden glory to
none but believers who have realized the soul's immortality.
In the old German folktales, swan-maidens wed earthly heroes,
but quit the earth the moment their husbands harbour the
slightest distrust. Lohengrin, swan-knight and guardian of
the Holy Grail, leaves Lady Elsa when she doubts and questions him.

The legends of Shakuntala and Parsifal, twin-currents of
romance, have sprung from the same fount of Indo-European
saga-lore.

offered the ring for sale in the bazaar.
When the goldsmith saw the royal initials
engraved on the gem, he took it to the
palace, and the indignant angler was
apprehended as a common thief. The
King, however, to the jeweller's astonishment, gave orders to acquit the fisherman,
and to reward the innocent man with a
handsome sum out of the royal treasury.

As soon as Dushyanta beheld the fatal
ring, his broken recollection was restored,
and his conjugal affection revived suddenly. Remorse and gloom now clouded
the Monarch's mind, and his infamous
desertion of Shakuntala burdened his conscience.

"When my darling with her antelope
eyes reminded me of our nuptials," he
lamented, "the links of my memory were
broken, and I basely rejected her without
a reasonable cause. But on seeing the
fatal gem I remembered everything, and
now I yearn for her sweet presence, and
cannot bear life, cut off as I am from her
dear companionship. Was it a dream that
impaired my memory, or an evil charm
that made me abandon her, or was my
unhappy forgetfulness the well-deserved

penance for sin committed in a previous
life? Well, whatever it was that confounded my judgment and obscured my
vision, I shall be plunged in lifelong
sorrow unless I find Shakuntala again.
When I think of her, how she fixed on
me her heavenly face, then deluged with
tears, I feel as if my heart were pierced
with a sharp iron. O my Shakuntala,
whom I have treated shamefully and forsaken unjustly, when will this vile traitor,
thy repentant husband, be once more
blessed with a sight of thee?"

Dushyanta's broken-heartedness was a
pleasing sacrifice in the eyes of Heaven,
and Indra, regent of the starry skies, sent
his celestial chariot, yoked with seven fiery
horses, to the despondent King that he
might also rise beyond terrestrial gloom.

Dushyanta gladly mounted the resplen-
dent car of the King of kings, and rapidly
ascended. The restless steeds rose high
above the ocean's vast expanse, and the
green, foam-crested waves were aflame
with the light of a thousand suns. Far
below, the Râja could see flights of cranes
ascend, in an ever-lengthening chain, from
fen and moor and meadow. And ever

higher was Dushyanta borne, beyond the
breezy heights where herds of musk-deer
wander, until he could no longer distin-
guish lowland valleys from high mountain
peaks. The vast river systems of India
spread out like a glittering net of silver
threads, and gigantic Himalay looked like
a pretty toy bridge cast from the eastern
to the western sea. The King rose higher
and higher. The sparkling steeds of Indra
had long traversed the region of the gold-
tinged clouds, when imperceptibly Dushyanta felt gently drawn back to earth.
No sooner came the feeling than like a
flash of lightning the radiant sun-car descended, and halted on the Hemakûta
Hills, now dipped in mellow evening light,
—the abode of holy ascetics.[1] Dushyanta,
glad to touch the solid earth again, sat
musing on a grey mossy stone by the side
of a steep rock. Close to him a beautiful
little boy was playing with a lion's whelp,
and the King heard him say:

" Open your mouth, baby-lion, I want
to count your teeth."

[1] The "snôwy heights" of Mount Meru, in the far north,
beyond wintry Himalay, were called Hemakûta; the name
signifies much the same as Snowdon or Mont Blanc. Chitra-
kûta, the scene of Râma's exile, means "picturesque heights".

"You naughty child," cried the nurse, "can't you leave the wild animals of the forest alone? Why do you torment them? The old lioness will tear you to pieces if you do not release her young one."

The boy bit his lip proudly, and answered defiantly: "I am not afraid of her."

Dushyanta felt strangely affected by the child's talk and appearance.

> "His brow is like the mountain snow
>   Gilt by the morning beam;
> His cheeks like living roses blow,
>   His eyes like azure stream."

"How happy must his father be," reflected the pensive King, "when this beautiful child sits by his side, playing with some toy, and prattling brightly, and laughing innocently at every trifling occurrence. Alas! I have no son to cheer my old age, and to perform, when I shall be no more, the funeral rites in my family. Yes, Puru's ancient race will die with me."

Again the old nurse was heard:

"Bharata dear, let the little lion go. I will give you something ever so much prettier to play with."

But young Bharata, with one hand pulling the lion by his mane, stretched out the other, saying:

"Give it first, nurse; in the meantime I will play with the lion."

The King had risen from his seat, and perchance seeing the palm of the boy's extended hand, beheld in the bold lines of its exquisite network the unmistakable signs of future eminence and kingship. The nurse now noticed Dushyanta, and courteously requested him to set the lion free from the grasp of this unmanageable child. The King reproved the boy:

"You, a pious hermit's son, how dare you disgrace your father by such cruelty, when you know that virtue on your part would make him happy? You ought to be ashamed to violate the rules of this consecrated forest. Only hideous black snakes infest the green boughs of a fragrant sandal tree."

The boy made no reply, but let the lion go. Gratified was the old nurse, as she curtsied and said:

"I thank you, gentle stranger, but our Bharata is not a hermit's son as you suppose. Upon my life, wonderful is the likeness between you and him, though you

are no relations. It also surprised me
to see how quickly you succeeded in restoring him to his natural good temper;
and yet the child has never seen you before."

Dushyanta felt a thrill of unknown joy
as he touched Bharata's curly head.

"Honourable dame, if the boy be not
a hermit's son, tell me what is his family
name?"

And the gladdening answer came back:

"He is King Dushyanta's child, and
his mother gave him birth in these hallowed woods."

The royal father, overjoyed at the happy
intelligence, fondly caressed his son, and
both went to the cottage to find the boy's
mother. But there she comes, in mourning weeds, to meet her darling child.
Pale are her lips, thin is her body, and
her dark, glossy hair is twisted in a single
braid.

"Forgive me," implored the King.
"Forgive! I have wronged you, but
tender love has now replaced hardness
of heart."

Shakuntala rejoiced — "Be confident,
my heart!" and answered quietly:

"I shall be most happy when the King's anger has passed away."

More she could not say; tears choked her voice. But the floodgates of Dushyanta's breast, so long pent up, burst open, and he cried passionately:

"My best-beloved, banish from your mind the thought of my cruel desertion of you. A violent frenzy had taken possession of my soul; but now, by the mercy of Heaven, thou bright day-star, I have found thee at last, sweet charmer, never to leave thee again."

And, sobbing, he fell at her feet.

"Rise, my husband! My happiness has long been interrupted, but now gladness dawns after the night of grief, since my dear lord still loves me."

Shakuntala's face shone as if the lights of Heaven were reflected in it when Dushyanta approached her. Fresh and sweet she looked like some mountain flower in which the dewdrops tremble at sunrise. Gently he wiped her tears away, and said:

"Thus I efface the memory of all tears which, in my dark hour, I have made thee shed."

And suddenly sweet light, bright colour,

rich scent, and floods of music filled the space, and Menaka, the radiant nymph, stood by their side.

"Yes, dear child," said she, "he always loved you. An imprecation obstructed the fountain of his love, but when he saw the fatal ring again, his loyal heart, dead to all else, was true to you. All this remained hidden from you by Indra's wise will, so that your wedded bliss might be the fuller and richer after your sore trials were ended. Hence cease, my son, to charge yourself with an offence which you committed unknowingly and therefore innocently."

"Then my name is cleared from infamy," rejoiced Dushyanta. And Menaka gave them a mother's holy blessing.

"My Shakuntala is the model of excellent wives, her son is dutiful, and thou, O King, hast three great advantages— true piety, abundant wealth, and practical benevolence. May the gods increase thy virtues and possessions a hundredfold!"

"Mother," said the King, "I now have reached the pinnacle of earthly bliss, and thy gracious benison gives assurance of happiness both to the Queen and myself.

First comes the flower, then the fruit;
friendly clouds gather before soft showers
fall; and even so thy kind favours precede
our felicity."

Shakuntala simply said:

"Happy am I that my lord who now
recognizes me has denied me through
ignorance, and not from real aversion."

Menaka then laid her right hand on
Bharata's young head.

"Thy heroic valour, my grandchild,
shall raise thee to overlordship stretching
from sea to sea, before thou shalt have
crossed the stormy ocean of this present
life.   Bharata is thy name, for thou shalt
rule unequalled in combat, and shalt support the fruitful earth." [1]

Dushyanta with his family returned to
Hastinapur, and during a long and beneficent reign consolidated and strengthened
the Empire, and promoted the welfare of
his subjects, who loved him for his wisdom
and justice, as they did Shakuntala for her
gentleness and acts of charity.

It was a time-hallowed custom among

---

[1] Bharat means "supporting" in Sanskrit, and is derived
from the same root as brother, i.e. supporter of the family
after the father's death.   Bhârata denotes a descendant of
Bharata.

the Princes of the royal house of Hastinapur, in the decline of life, to leave their
gilded palaces with marble columns and
stuccoed walls, and seek humbler mansions
in the quiet forest, under spreading trees
or in secluded caves, and henceforth to
dedicate themselves to austerities and to
the service of Heaven.

" Forsaking worldly cares in life's decline,
  Hastina's kings sceptre and throne resign;
  Assume the garment of the holy sage,
  And spend in thoughts of God their tranquil age."

When the time had come, Dushyanta, full
of years, and ripe in knowledge, accom-
panied by Shakuntala, now a venerable
matron, repaired to St. Kanva's hermitage.
Kanva was long dead, but St. Shârngarava,
being Superior of the holy confraternity,
joyfully received the King and Queen;
and there they stayed, practising yoga and
reading the holy shâstras, until the course
of their earthly days was run.[1]

[1] The old Sanskrit books record several instances of crowned
heads abandoning the splendour and allurements of a gay Court
for the more congenial seclusion in the vana-prastha or forest-
upland. In a peaceful hermitage they became absorbed in the
contemplation of the divine mysteries,—the uplifted heart par-
taking of God's very self in yoga or interior communion. The
kingly bearing and fearless spirit of the vânaprasthas or forest

The crown of Hastinapur had devolved
on Bharata the hero-king, and his descendants were the warlike Bhârata race, renowned in battle, who played such a
prominent part in the subsequent history
of India during the Heroic Age. Their
deadly family feuds, and especially the
great war waged on the plains of Kuru-
kshetra between the Kauravas and Pân-
davas, two mighty brother tribes, have been
sung by many a minstrel, in many a popular ballad, in the baronial banquet halls
of ancient Hindustan. But the story of
Shakuntala, the common mother of the
Bhâratas, fell into oblivion for lack of a
great troubadour, until, ages hence, Kâlidâsa was born, sweet singer of Ujain, who
made Shakuntala the subject of a melodious
Sanskrit play.

Kâlidâsa has long descended to his cold
tomb. According to a tradition, the poet

hermits, whose beaming eyes shone with the light of God,
excited the admiration of Alexander the Great. The royal
enthusiast who prized Pindar's lofty strains above earthly
music felt the subtle charm of lowly âshrams, the sweet haunt
of all the Muses. But the mighty ruler, though accustomed to
universal homage, tried in vain to engage some of the Indian
munis (recluses) in spiritual converse. Like the Carthusian
monks in Western lands, the God-illumined munis observed
perpetual silence in their simple woodland retreat.

lies buried on a lonely hill in balmy Ceylon,
within hearing of the surging ocean's roar.
Forgotten is the site of his green grave;
maybe, wild roses bloom even now on it,
and the mountain deer which he loved so
well graze on it in the spicy morning breeze.
But not forgotten is his deathless lay. Hail
to thee, Kâlidâsa, Prince among poets,
who still thrillest our souls with thy immortal song of sweet Shakuntala!

5. Has Greece Influenced the Indian Theatre?

The origin of the Hindu theatre is
wrapped in darkness, and, until fresh evidence be brought to light, the best theory
offered is that Kâlidâsa perfected, whereas
his forerunners created the Sanskrit drama
out of the lost Prâkrit plays, including the
sanvâdas or mysteries which were enacted
at solemn seasons of periodic sacrifice.
Vedic and epic bards alike, as well as the
later dramatists, must have felt that Sanskrit
was a fitter vehicle than Prâkrit for express-
ing profound thoughts and sublime sentiments, and stood a better chance of survival
than current speech which follows the

changing taste and fashion. Yet, there
are well-read scholars who maintain that
India has borrowed the drama from Greece.
Ever since the days of Alexander the Great,
Greek colonies were thriving at the seaports
and trading stations of the East. It is quite
possible that these settlements of wealthy
Greeks kept up a native stage so that
they might beguile a few hours pleasantly,
after a busy day, just as English officers
and civilians frequent the performances of
the Simla Dramatic Club. Ujain and
Kanouj, where the early Sanskrit theatre
took root and flourished, may have come
in contact with Greek trade and culture,
nay, Kâlidâsa and Bâna had perhaps some
acquaintance with Attic wit and letters.
Even if all these assumptions were correct,
although there is no real basis for them,
still the classical theatre of the Hindus
would have a just claim to originality.
The *Merchant of Venice* is not a mere
imitation of an old Italian novel, nor is
Goethe's *Iphigenia* borrowed from Euri-
pides, nor La Fontaine's fables from an
Eastern source. Genius never copies
slavishly, although foreign ideas may
awaken a congenial strain in the tuneful

breast.   But no direct proof whatever can
be adduced that any Hellenic influence was
brought to bear upon the Indian drama,
which has a thoroughly national foundation.   On the contrary, there are weighty
reasons for disbelieving in such influences,
for Greek and Hindu plays diametrically
differ both in arrangement and principle.
The Greeks recognize, whereas the author
of Shakuntala ignores the unity of time
and place.   The Greek chorus, in the
character of a moral judge, is entirely unknown in his productions.   On the other
hand, the happy blending of tragic and
comic incidents, which is characteristic of
Indian quite as much as of Shakespearean
plays, is altogether against the rules of the
Athenian stage.   The keynote of Greek
poetry is joy and pride of life, but Sanskrit
dramas, though they all end well, generally
moralize on the text that life is but vanity
and vexation of spirit.

On these internal grounds we contend
that the Indian theatre is home-grown,
and not a foreign graft.   If epic and lyric
matured into the drama under Greek skies,
why could not Sanskrit literature have
passed through a similar process of evolu-

tion? The same sun ripens fruit and corn in Orient and Occident. Does it necessarily follow that American wheat must have been transplanted from Russian soil because it was cultivated in the Mississippi valley later than in the fertile plains of the Volga? or that the German theatre is a Chinese loan because playhouses existed in Peking ever so much earlier than in Leipzig and Weimar? The human mind, given similar conditions, shows the same tendencies and possibilities everywhere, and if dramatic literature originated independently in China and in Greece, well, the same could have happened in India.

6. King Shûdraka

Shakuntala is the daintiest and most graceful of all Sanskrit plays, but the most powerful on the stage is *The Toy Cart*, which was composed in the reign of King Shûdraka, about the sixth century.[1] The unknown author, who enjoyed the royal patronage, gives a graphic picture of social life in medieval India.[2]

[1] Native tradition ascribes the authorship to Shûdraka. *The Toy Cart* was merely dedicated to the King.

[2] The beauties of spring, matchless like maiden's charms,

Âryaka, a young herdsman, had been apprehended and imprisoned by order of King Pâlaka. The Râja, like Krishna's royal kinsman, was troubled because of a prophecy that a shepherd dynasty was to overthrow his own. Pâlaka was a tyrant, and Sansthânaka, the Queen's brother, was a spendthrift and a libertine. One day the debauched Prince molested the beautiful Lady Vasanta, who had been shopping in the bazaar. She took refuge in Chârudatta's house, and begged the poor but virtuous brahmin to protect her against the insolent and vulgar addresses of the unprincipled Sansthânaka. Evening drew near, and as the streets were unsafe at

have suggested such names as May, Violet, or Lily in England, and Mâlati (jasmine) or Vasanta (vernal season) in India. The heroine of *The Toy Cart* is called Vasantasena in the original, but we have taken the liberty to shorten the polysyllable. No doubt, clipped Sanskrit jars on the ears of Oriental scholars, and the only apology we can offer for the various abbreviations introduced in this volume is the convenience of short names, and their consonance with English taste and usage. Phil and Bess are more popular than Philip and Elizabeth, while bus and bike and taxi are quite colloquial expressions. What does it matter after all of how many syllables a word is composed as long as the speaker clearly conveys his meaning? Language is not the only department in nature where form after form is broken up for the sake of adaptation to new environments. All created forms and names are bound to pass through successive stages of growth and decay. Decomposition leads to reconstruction in the revolving cycle of things manifest.

night, Vasanta left her jewellery in the
brahmin's charge, and gladly accepted his
offer to escort her home.

Soon after, Sharvilaka left Vasanta's
house. He kept company with the lady's
maid, and dearly wished to purchase the
freedom of the slave-girl, so that they
might get married. But then he was only
a poor working man, and how could he
possibly raise a sufficient sum of money?
Such were his anxious thoughts when he
suddenly overheard the words — "and
thank you so much for taking care of my
jewels; I am sure to send for them to-
morrow morning". The person addressed
was Chârudatta. Sharvilaka followed him
unnoticed, and when the priest entered his
humble home, the thief managed to glide
after him into the dark passage. There
he waited until all was quiet. It was after
midnight that Sharvilaka, with noiseless
step and bated breath, felt his way to the
bedroom, where, after some search, he hit
on the coveted treasure, and made off
with it.

Next morning, Chârudatta was in great
consternation. If he told the truth, and
stated that burglars had broken into a

poor brahmin's house, who would believe him? No; let her rather think of him as a reckless than a dishonest man. So he pretended to have gambled away the entrusted deposit; and wishing to refund the loss to the best of his power, he offered Vasanta his wife's necklace, old-fashioned, but of considerable value. It was the only ornament left to the poor woman. Everything else had long been sold for life's bare necessities.

Sharvilaka, in high glee, related to his sweetheart the adventures of the preceding night. The honest girl was shocked to hear of the theft, and told her lover that she would have no more to do with him until he had restored what she knew belonged to her mistress. Sharvilaka, conscience-stricken and henpecked at the same time, gave up the stolen property, and the maid took the jewels to their rightful owner, with a message that the parcel had been left for Her Ladyship.

But walls have ears. The conversation of the two had come to Vasanta's knowledge, and being pleased with the upright conduct of her maid, she gave her a handsome present in money, and permission to

get married.   Good had come out of evil,
and Sharvilaka was a happy man when
he learned his good fortune.   He came to
thank Vasanta, and parted with a grateful heart to make the necessary preparations for the wedding.   As he opened the
front door, a man rushed in, gasping for
breath, and anxiously looking for a place
of concealment.   He had lost every su-
varna, he said, and had run away from the
gaming table when he could pay no longer;
but now the other gamesters were hard at
his heels, and if they caught him he would
have to go to jail unless his debts were
paid.   No person in distress ever appealed
in vain to the generous Vasanta.   She at
once satisfied the claims of the importunate
creditors.   The relieved gambler took a
solemn vow to give up his disreputable
life, and entered a Buddhist monastery.

Vasanta was deeply touched by Chârudatta's disinterested diplomacy, and had
humour enough to fall in with his delicate
tactics.   So she made up a mournful
tale, and acknowledged that she too was
addicted to gambling, and had recklessly
staked the necklace of the brahmin's wife.
" But alas! I lost," speaking with down-

cast eyes, and heaving a gentle sigh. The lady then handed Chârudatta a jewel box, which she begged him to accept in the meantime. On opening the casket the astonished priest recognized the stolen gems, and the mystery of their recovery was speedily cleared up amid much mirth and laughter. The interview ended with mutual assurances of goodwill and love.[1]

As Vasanta was chatting with the brahmin's wife, his youngest boy came running into the room. The little fellow cried piteously; he was tired of playing with his toy cart of burnt clay, and wanted golden playthings such as the son of the rich neighbour had. Vasanta longed to help her impoverished friends without giving offence, which the poor take so easily, and gladly turned the little incident to practical account. Patting the child's head fondly, she gave him a handful of jewels, and said: "Ask dadda to sell these stones, and buy you a toy cart of gold." She then left hurriedly, and the lad stood gazing at the glittering stones with wondering joy.

[1] We have divested Vasanta of all levity and laxity which the reader might attribute to her character, if, in agreement with the Sanskrit text, she had been represented as a refined courtesan like Aspasia of Greece.

During this pretty family scene Sansthâ-naka was paying a call next door, where the rich folks lived. His palanquin waited outside, and Vasanta, mistaking it for her own, stepped into the vehicle. The bearers, being under the impression that it was the Prince who had entered, moved on to the deer park as usual.

That very day Âryaka, by the help of his friend Sharvilaka, had escaped from the prison cell. No sooner was the flight discovered than a hue and cry was raised, and a hot pursuit began all over the city. The game was well-nigh up; the fugitive expected to be rearrested every moment. How could he baffle the keen-scented police? Bewildered, he dashed past Châru-datta's house, when, by a lucky chance, Âryaka noticed Vasanta's palanquin. If he only succeeded in putting the blood-hounds off the right track! Desperate and regardless of all consequences, the hunted man slipped unobserved into the empty conveyance, and drew the curtain. Vasanta's slaves, never suspecting that they did not carry their mistress, bore Âryaka to her house, where Sharvilaka's girl concealed the exhausted herdsman.

The next to appear on the scene was
the King's brother-in-law. When he could
not find his carriage, he flew into a passion, and walked off at last, swaggering
and swearing loudly. Sansthânaka did
not much like to be seen on foot by his
fashionable friends, so he cut right across
the deer park to the deserted lake at
the other end. There the ex-gambler,
now a devout Buddhist, was washing
his yellow robe. Without the slightest
provocation the vicious Prince knocked
the harmless monk down, but his vile and
cruel temper quickly passed into a fresh
channel at the unexpected sight of his
palanquin. Sansthânaka called out to the
startled liverymen, and poured on them a
volley of threatening language and abuse.
But on beholding Vasanta, "he gave a
whistle long and low", and put his arms
round her waist. Disgusted and terrified,
she pushed him away; he stumbled, and
measured his full length upon the ground.
The ruffian got up again, and, white with
rage, dragged the unfortunate lady out of
the carriage. After dismissing the atten-
dants abruptly, he struck her in the face,
and beat her mercilessly until life seemed

extinct. But Sansthânaka was as cowardly
as he was depraved. Trembling, he looked
about lest somebody should have witnessed
his misdeeds. But there was no sign of
a human being anywhere. The monster
hastily scraped a large heap of dry leaves
together, threw them over Vasanta's body,
and decamped. In the distance he noticed
Chârudatta absorbed in thought, but to
the guilty conscience of Sansthânaka it
seemed as though the detested priest had
watched him.

Vasanta was not dead, but stunned by
the heavy blows she had received. As
soon as her assailant was gone the Buddhist monk, still faint from loss of blood,
came up, and charitably busied himself in
reviving his fellow-victim from her death-
like swoon. He fetched water, bathed her
wounds, and ministered to all her needs,
the more tenderly when he recognized his
never-forgotten benefactress.

Sansthânaka bore Chârudatta a secret
grudge ever since the priest had offered
protection to Vasanta and had foiled his
evil intentions. The infamous Prince was
afraid of being reported, and, at the same
time, anxious to ruin his hated adversary.

He seized the golden opportunity, and
with a bold front accused the innocent
brahmin of Vasanta's murder. Chârudatta
was sent for, and calmly denied the charge.
He was so beloved in the city that nobody
in the court really believed him capable of
the dastardly crime. Yet Chârudatta had
to admit that he had been near the lake at
the hour when, according to the indict-
ment, the murder was committed. Moreover, Vasanta had been seen in defendant's
house on her dying day. Besides, she was
rich, while he was poor, and it would not
have been the first time that poverty led
to crime. Another link in the chain of
appearances against Chârudatta was that
his informer was the Queen's brother, a
man of the highest rank and influence.
The kindly judge looked grave as he
gave orders to have the indicated place
searched for the dead body. When no
trace of it could be found, Sansthânaka
declared on oath that he had seen the
priest murder the woman, and after the
foul deed despoil her of all jewellery.
"How am I to know what has happened
to the corpshe?" he replied sullenly to
the interrogating judge; "the villain

might have thrown it in the pond for aught
I know."[1]

Just then Maitreya, the happy-go-lucky
jester in the play, passed the law courts on
his way home; he lived within a stone's
throw of Vasanta's house. His friend
Chârudatta had begged him to take the
jewels back to the lady, who was evidently
in a playful mood when she gave them to
his little boy. Maitreya was fond of gossip,
and as he was not in a particular hurry (he
never was), he entered the courts to see
what was going on. Good Heavens! there
stood his venerable friend, accused of man-
slaughter. Maitreya could not believe it.
On hearing the details, he was unable to
restrain his angry passion, and violently
denounced Sansthânaka before the assembled court. Had he not seen with his
own eyes, but two days ago, how that
scoundrel of a Prince annoyed and insulted

[1] The Prince's vulgar language is quite in harmony with his
low character. Like the Shaka hordes who adopted a "decadent" prâkrit when they overran India, *Shansh*thânaka cannot
pronounce the letter *s* properly, much as a peasant lad of
*Sh*ligo or an illiterate German in New York is *sh*low to under-
*sh*tand the full value of English sounds. Moreover, Va*sh*anta's
loathed admirer affects a taste for literature which is utterly
foreign to his base sentiments, and constantly parades his
ignorance by misquoting the national epics.

Vasanta publicly in the street? And was not Chârudatta respected by every townsman for his lofty principles and spotless character? In his excitement Maitreya dropped the jewels, which he was holding under his robe for safety. They were at once identified as Vasanta's property, and Maitreya was arrested on the charge of complicity. Defendant was again cross-examined, and owned that he had handed the incriminating gems to his apparent accomplice. On this additional evidence the jury convicted Chârudatta, and banished him for life. Before the Mohammedan Conquest, reverend brahmins, whatever their crime might be, were exempt from capital punishment. But King Pâlaka took the law into his own hand in Chârudatta's case. Although the Râja had little cause to trust any statement made by his worthless brother-in-law, he was more averse to the publicity of a Court scandal than to the infliction of a grievous wrong. Determined, at all costs, to save the honour of the royal family, the despot not only accepted without question the verdict (though he thought there might have been a miscarriage of justice), but even aggravated

the legal sentence, and signed the con-
demned man's death warrant. Human respect had stifled the voice of Pâlaka's
conscience.

Chârudatta was wonderfully resigned. He
looked serene and dignified as the jailers
led him to the place of execution. The
chandâla was ready to strike the fatal blow
when suddenly Vasanta and her Buddhist
friend forced their way through the surging
crowd, and begged a moment's hearing.
The lady had been ill all the time; only
this morning the horrible news was conveyed to her sick-bed. And now she was
here to bear witness to the truth that the
priest was innocent, and his accuser guilty.

The bloodthirsty rabble listened to
Vasanta's thrilling tale in deep silence. It
was the lull before a storm. "Let His
Majesty's orders be carried into effect; put
the culprit to death, him of blood royal,"
was the general outcry. Sansthânaka, who
had invited a "smart set" of friends to
attend the execution, grew deadly pale.
Chârudatta, in a firm and ringing voice,
then entreated the people to listen for a
moment. When the wild turmoil subsided,
he forgave his persecutor, and, with tears

in his eyes, pleaded for the Prince's forfeited life.

"Long live the noble Âryaka!" "Prosperity to King Âryaka!" the burghers
shouted in the streets. The old prophecy
had come true at last. King Pâlaka lay
assassinated in his palace for disregarding
the ancient law of the land. Âryaka, whose
undeserved misfortunes had aroused general
sympathy, was solemnly crowned amid the
enthusiastic acclamations of the populace.
The new Monarch's first gracious act was
to nominate Chârudatta Governor of a province, and give him Lady Vasanta in marriage.   Bigamy is not held criminal in
India, although monogamy, less costly to
the husband, is the rule amongst the middle
classes.   The ex-gambler was appointed
Superior-General of the Buddhist monasteries throughout the country, and Sharvilaka, the reformed thief, Chief of the City
Police.[1]

[1] The most recent translation of the play is by W. Ryder
(Cambridge, Mass., 1905, $1.50).—Why does not an enter-
prising theatrical manager produce in cosmopolitan New York
or London the best of the world's dramatic literature? Masterpieces like Goethe's *Egmont*, Calderon's *Judge of Zalamea*, or
Shûdraka's *Toy Cart*, if only staged and paraphrased well, are
sure to be appreciated by large and enthusiastic audiences.

7. Kâlidâsa Again

Soon after Alexander's death, the vast dominions which had been subject to his rule were dismembered, for he had dreamt, no less than the great Corsican, of world-wide conquest rather than of a federated empire. Oriental romance endowed Iskander—that is the Persian name of Philip's warlike son—with magical gifts and super-human virtues. In the third century B.C., when the Greek dependencies in the East were no longer held together by Iskander's wondrous personality, huge fragments of conquered territory broke off the Imperial colossus, and were tossed about like so many tennis balls between usurper and conspirator. Bactria, a Macedonian colony in Turkestan, alone stood firm and grew powerful, despite all political schemes and diplomatic intrigues. It was owing to the military genius of Seleucus, one of Iskander's ablest lieutenants, that Bactrian rule came to extend from the Syrian Sea to the Indian border. The Seleucides, that is, the successors of Seleucus, erected strong forts along the river Indus, and occupied

Gujarat. Ashoka's son or grandson, being fully awake to the danger which threatened Magadha if the Greek regiments marched further east, sent General Pushpamitra against the foreign invader. Pushpamitra attacked and defeated the Bactrian forces somewhere in the Punjab, and returned home. laden with rich spoil and trophies. His Indian countrymen gave him a splendid reception, and fêted him as a national hero, while the victorious troops were vociferously cheered in every town and village through which they passed. Popular sentiment ran high at Patna, where the gallant field-marshal received honours and ovations befitting an emperor or king. Popularity is apt to rouse slumbering ambition, and the native chroniclers relate that about B.C. 180 Pushpamitra overthrew the dynasty of Chandragupta, and succeeded to the Imperial Crown of Magadha.

Pushpamitra's son and successor was Agnimitra, whose suzerainty was acknowledged as far south as Nagpur, where Mâdhava reigned just then. The powerful Râja of Berar had forcibly annexed the little state of Nagpur. King Mâdhava, on offering resistance, was made a prisoner of war. Princess Kaushiki of Nagpur and her beautiful sister Mâlavika fled in disguise, and joined a travelling caravan which was bound for the capital of Magadha. But alas! a gang of highwaymen waylaid and robbed the traders. The brigands carried Mâlavika off to the Patna slave market, where the attractive girl was purchased for the seraglio of Queen Dhârini. The heavy chain of family misfortunes weighed upon Kaushiki's depressed spirits, and the royal maid, desirous of propitiating dire fate, vowed she would take the veil, and become a Buddhist nun, if ever she reached Magadha safely. In the meantime, Agnimitra's armies marched against Berar to King Mâdhava's rescue.

Such is the historical background of one of Kâlidâsa's plays. The drama is much admired in India, but is inferior, and probably also anterior, to Shakuntala.

Agnimitra falls in love with Mâlavika's portrait, which he has seen in the Queen's apartments. Dhârini is jealous, and takes good care to keep the original out of the King's sight. He consults his vidûshaka or Court jester as to the possibility of an interview with Mâlavika. Gautama—that

is the confidant's name — raises a great
argument between the singing master and
dancing instructor of the seraglio, and the
result is a lively quarrel as to their respective merits. Lovers of Molière's muse will
be reminded of the humorous scene where
Mons. Jourdain's tutors in fencing and
music pass from light words to heavy
blows. The politic Gautama pretends to
be seriously alarmed at the heated dispute;
he advises to refer the controversy to His
Majesty, and have it amicably settled.
The royal arbiter, in his turn, proposes
a sangîta or competitive ballet-concert in
which the best pupils are to take part.
The sangîta is held accordingly. Mâlavika
dances the most difficult steps with perfect
ease and beauty. Brilliant is her technique, and full of grace each movement.
The enchanted Râja does not take his eye
off Mâlavika during the whole performance,
and in the end awards the prize to the
elated dancing master. The maiden's fur-
tive glances intimate sufficiently that the
King's tenderness is not unrequited. An
appointment is made, the vidûshaka acting
again as go-between. But the Queen's
unexpected arrival interrupts unpleasantly

the sweet *tête-à-tête* and the stolen kisses
of the amorous couple. A scene is happily
avoided by the joyful intelligence, brought
at an opportune moment, of a decisive
victory which the Imperialists have gained,
and of Mâdhava's successful deliverance.
Her Majesty is still undecided whether to
rebuke or congratulate the Râja when another messenger arrives from the northern
highlands.

" His secret mission told,
The fragrant scroll is speedily unrolled ",

and conveys the glad tidings that the
Crown Prince, after heroic efforts, has sub-
jugated one of the most turbulent hill tribes.
Dhârini feels less inclined than ever to up-
braid the King.   The threatening clouds
vanish entirely from the domestic horizon
when a special embassy bears costly presents from the submissive Râja of Berar
for King Agnimitra and his Queen.   There
is a fine curved sabre, its handsome hilt
emblazoned with studs of purest gold, and
a superb arrow-case richly inlaid with precious stones.   There are flower-embroidered
silks and gaudy shawls of Berar make,
circlets sparkling with diamonds, and a

couple of cream-coloured donkeys. Two
Nagpur bayaderes of exquisite skill and
beauty are to divert the ladies of the royal
zenana with dance and song. The nautch
girls utter a cry of unfeigned surprise as
they recognize in Mâlavika one of their lost
Princesses. Dhârini is in a forgiving and
generous mood because of the military
triumphs of her darling son; moreover,
she is gratified with the lovely presents.
Her gracious consent is not withheld when
Agnimitra confers on Mâlavika the title
of a Sub-Queen; she is to be the Râja's
rightful bride. Mâlavika's strange adventures are the talk of Magadha, and even
reach the peaceful convent cell of Sister
Kaushiki. She is overjoyed, and hastens
to the palace. The curtain falls over the
sobs and kisses of the reunited sisters.

.   .   .   .

Kâlidâsa has also written a romantic
opera, which would draw crowded houses
to Covent Garden if a gifted composer set
it to effective music.

The mermaid Urvashi is wedded to King
Purûravas. Like a river that bursts its
banks in spring, she has trespassed on the
grounds of Uma's warrior son. The irate

god transforms the fair offender into a slender vine.[1] The King, frantic with grief, wanders over hill and dale, in search of the beloved nymph.   He enquires piteously, even of the dumb creation, whether they have not seen her pass.

> " I will speak to the peacock.   O tell
> If—free on the wings as you soar—
> In forest or meadow or dell
> You have seen the loved nymph I adore.
> You will know her, the fairest of damsels fair,
> By her large soft eyes and her graceful air."

But the conceited bird disdains to listen to other people's troubles, and haughtily displays his gorgeous plumage.   Purûravas reflects that the boastful creature cannot have seen his love, whose beautiful tresses would have put his painted feathers to shame.   He walks on, and comes to a forest lake.   Tranquilly a swan glides over the still waters.   The elegant movements of the bird arrest the King's attention; the hansa can only have copied them from dainty Urvashi.

---

[1] The legend, which is located in Kurukshetra, is the subject of a popular sanvâda ballad in the Rig Veda (X, 95). Kâlidâsa's opera and his Shakuntala are based alike on old Indian folklore.

" If thou hadst never seen her graceful form,
  Straying along the flower-tufted bank,
  Then whence this elegant gait? 't is hers, and thou
  Hast stolen it from her in whose every step
  Love sports. Thy walk betrays thee. Own thy
      theft,
  And lead me quickly to her."

But the swan moves on unconcerned, and
leaves the royal questioner to his melancholy thoughts. The orchestra plays a
tender and pensive air.[1] A swarm of wild
bees is buzzing over a tangle of yellow
lotuses. The King's reverie is again interrupted, and he soliloquizes:

" How beautiful the lotus! it arrests
  My path, and bids me gaze on it. The bees
  Murmur against its petals. Like the lips
  Of my beloved it glows when they have been
  Somewhat too rudely sipped by mine, and sweetly
  Protest against such violence."

[1] The swan-motif may well be a poet's reminiscence of the
swan-maidens, to whom Vedic romance is no less partial than
English and German folklore. Swan-breasted clouds, pregnant
with genial showers, sail over the blue summer sky, or, in the
language of mythology, lovely swan-maidens, with sunlit eyes
and faces rosy-hued, float blithely in the azure lakes of Indra's
gay-tinted heaven. Swan-bosomed Urvashi and her seductive
sisters gleam with golden ringlets and flowing silvery veils.
Like refreshing rain, much needed, the bewitching cloud-sisters
descend from heaven to earth, as did the mother of Shakuntala
to console her forsaken child. The mountain lakes wherein the
lissom apsarases or mermaids bathe and sport were originally
not terrestrial waters, but signified celestial phenomena,

The lonesome wanderer turns to one of the silver-winged sailors on the scent-laden breeze:

"Sweet plunderer of the honeyed dew, hast thou
    Beheld the nymph with large and languid eyes?
    The rippling wave is like her arching brow,
    The fluttering line of storks her timid tongue,
    The foamy spray her white loose-floating vest."
                    [*Speaking to himself.*
"And yet, methinks, it's idle to enquire,
    For had he tasted her delicious breath,
    He now would scorn the lotus."

At last the goddess Uma takes pity on the royal sufferings. She places in the Râja's way a ruby stone endowed with the virtue of disenchanting the metamorphosed nymph. Purûravas exclaims:

"What stream of ruddy radiance breaks
Through the cleft rock?   No flame could have survived
The fast-descending floods.   Is it perhaps
Some sanguine fragment of a lion's feast?
No, 't is a gem more roseate than the blush
Of rhododendron blossoms."

A celestial voice speaks from on high:

"Take up the gem, my son.   Its radiant red
    Adorn thy hand, restore to thee thy bride!"

The distracted lover takes up the magic

stone, and feels irresistibly drawn to a climbing vine.

> " What means this strange emotion as I gaze
> Upon this vine?   No blossoms deck her boughs,
> No bees regale her with soft music.   Sad
> And silent is the lonely plant, the image
> Of my repentant love.   O let me press
> The melancholy likeness to my breast."

The warm touch of affection thrills through every fibre of the trembling creeper, and changes it back to human form.   Urvashi lies weeping in the arms of Purûravas.   Is there magic more wonderful than the magic of true and tender love?[1]

[1] The poetical quotations are taken from Wilson's translation.—Purûravas resembles the lover in the English folksong:

> " O red rose in the garden,
>   O red rose on the spray,
> Saw you my maiden beautiful
>   Pass hither on her way?

> " Perchance she kissed your petals,
>   And turned from white to red
> The rose that blushed to find itself
>   With fairer sweets o'erspread."

When the rose withholds an answer, the sentimental youth questions blackbird and nightingale whether they have not seen his lady-love; from her dulcet voice alone they could have caught such sweet and plaintive notes:

> " O blackbird in the thicket,
>   And you, sad nightingale,
> Heard you my maiden beautiful
>   Go singing down the vale?"

Shakespeare, too, upbraids the forward violets for having stolen sweet fragrance from maiden's breath. and from her veins their purple pride.

8. The Drama in King Harsha's Reign

More people are helped by reading the *Vicar of Wakefield* than the *Origin of Species*. Philosophic truth appeals to the reasoning faculties of a few only, but the contemplation of a good and useful life goes straight to the human heart. The same reflection applies to Indian literature. Even amongst educated Hindus not many will be found who have a clear notion of Sânkhya psychology, but there is hardly a village school throughout the length and breadth of the land where the native children are not familiar with some version of Shakuntala.

The muse of poetry had lavishly bestowed her choicest gifts on Kâlidâsa, and his responsive soul poured forth an abundance of melodious song. Poets and poetasters eagerly cultivated Kâlidâsa's style, but none of their productions has survived. Even the cleverest imitations are mediocre and ephemeral; only original ideas can stand the critical test of time. The first half of the seventh century witnessed a fresh outburst of dramatic activity among the Hindus, and RATNÂVALI, or THE PEARL NECKLACE, is generally considered the best drama of that period. Bâna, whom most pundits believe to be the author, presided over the republic of letters during King Harsha's reign with the same dignity and distinction as Dr. Johnson did under the Georges.[1]

Ratnâvali, Princess of Ceylon, has suffered shipwreck on a shallow sandbank off the Indian coast. She is happily rescued and taken ashore, without, however, divulging her illustrious lineage. The beautiful and accomplished girl is presently introduced to Queen Vâsavadatta, who engages her for the royal zenana. It is here that King Vatsa meets Ratnâvali, and is won by her seductive charms. Tender words and softer glances are exchanged between the two. The uneasy Queen, in a dry and peremptory tone, commands Ratnâvali to go and fetch her parrot from the aviary.

The next act shows the heroine reposing on a sloping lawn in Vâsavadatta's garden. She holds a blue-necked parrot by a silver

[1] For King Harsha and his reign, see *Short History of Indian Literature*, chapters xii and xvii.

chain, and seems in a pensive mood. After a while, the lady changes her reclining posture and begins sketching with coloured earth. Ratnâvali is so absorbed in her artistic work that she does not notice Susangata, another maid-of-honour, who approaches on tiptoe from behind, and playfully lays her hand over the eyes of her sentimental friend. On seeing King Vatsa's flattered portrait, which is nearly finished, Susangata saucily snatches up the drawing from Ratnâvali's lap, and with a practised hand pencils hastily the fair painter's face by the side of the portrayed King. Ratnâvali is exceedingly annoyed, and wants to recover the painting. During the struggle which ensues, the chain slips off her fingers. The parrot, only too glad to regain sweet liberty, takes wing, and perches on a leafy bough in the adjacent orangery. The two maidens, flushed with excitement, run after the Queen's pet bird, no longer heeding the object of their squabble.

Just then, the Monarch and his jester had a stroll in the gardens, and happened to pass the spot where the unfinished sketch lay exposed on the ground. Vatsa looked

at it earnestly; his fluttering heart told him
that Ratnâvali had drawn it, and that she
must be in love with him. In the meantime the damsels came back to fetch their
things from the garden seat. On hearing
men's voices, they hid behind a thick-
clustered jasmine bush. The Râja, unaware of their presence, praised Ratnâvali's
goodness and beauty in enraptured terms.
No sooner had Susangata heard the royal
declaration of love than, with an arch twinkle
in her roguish eyes, she dragged forth her
blushing companion, "whose tulip cheek
with deeper crimson glowed". The shrewd
maiden then skilfully engaged the talkative
jester, who was a zealous botanist, in an
engrossing conversation on horticultural
topics; he was to tell her all the Sanskrit
names of the newly-arrived plants in the
shrubbery. The lovers were left alone.
They felt embarrassed at first, but soon
recovered from their nervousness. It
was arranged that Ratnâvali, disguised as
Vâsavadatta, should visit the King in the
evening.

The concerted plot was ingenious, but
the lady-detectives of the jealous Rani were
watching and eavesdropping everywhere.

They soon discovered Vatsa's latest intrigue, and confirmed Vâsavadatta's worst fears and suspicions. The perturbed Queen restrained her just anger; she would quietly wait her turn, and entangle the royal fowler in the net which he had cast. She meant to anticipate the new rival in her affections and go herself to Vatsa in the gloaming.

How ardently the Râja welcomed his beautiful spouse, whom he mistook for the little rosebud Ratnâvali! Her disguise was so perfect, he said, that in the dusk his lovely guest looked every inch the real Queen. Vâsavadatta was careful not to dispel the King's illusion, and unmask the traitor, until the measure of his perfidy was full. She kept her face veiled, and refrained from speaking. Vatsa, made eloquent by what seemed to him maidenly bashfulness, repeated more than once how passionately he loved Ratnâvali. "Since your bright star has risen on the horizon of my heart, beloved, even fair Vâsavadatta shines with a fainter light." The Rani trembled with stifled rage, and could hardly control her sorely tried temper, but she would hear the end of it. The King, misinterpreting her tremulous silence for coyness and reserve,

gently drew the sweet face to his breast, and
called her all those pretty names which
love's folly suggests. That was too much
for poor Vâsavadatta; in a paroxysm of
grief she tore herself from the arms of her
unfaithful lord, sobbing and crying bitterly.
However fickle Vatsa was, he loved his
consort, and implored her to forgive him.
But the insulted wife proudly drew up her
queenly form to its full height, and, quickly
drying her tears, left the King without a
single word either of pardon or reproach.
Vatsa felt mortified, and wished that he
had never met Ratnâvali. He must have
given utterance to the painful thought within
hearing of bright-eyed Ratnâvali, who
blithely tripped along on her stolen errand
of love just then, for with a troubled coun-
tenance and a hurried step the maiden withdrew from the royal presence before the
King had even noticed her.

Her dejected appearance caused grave
anxiety to His Majesty's jester whom she
passed. The good-hearted fool, being
under the impression that it was the Queen
whom he had met, was much concerned
about her, and followed at a respectful distance, to be of help if needed. Ratnâvali

hastened through the palace grounds into the open fields. In a fit of despair she threw herself on the ground, muttering incoherent words, and showing signs of mental distraction. The horrified vidûshaka ran back and informed Vatsa that the Rani was about to commit suicide. The repentant Râja rushed out to save the dear life, but what a wild conflict of feelings surged in his agitated breast when he found, instead of the Queen, Ratnâvali bathed in a flood of tears! In her present affliction she looked even lovelier than in her happy mood a few hours since. All his good resolutions melted away before the warmth of his affection as snow before the summer sun, and Vatsa kissed the tears away from the cheeks of his beloved.

Vâsavadatta, too, felt conscience-stricken after the distressing interview with Vatsa. Had she not been too harsh and hasty with her royal mate? This very moment she would go back and make it up with him! On her way to his private apartments she met the vidûshaka, who was delighted to see her safe and hale once more. At the same time, the jester was puzzled at her eager enquiry for the King. Vatsa, then,

had not found her after all? The simple
fool wonderingly pointed to the fields
where he had witnessed the agony of the
pseudo-Queen. Vâsavadatta followed the
indicated direction. How she longed for
the blissful moment of reconciliation, and
for the restoration of domestic happiness!
Her love of Vatsa, and her desire to be at
peace with him, lent wings to her graceful
steps. She came nearer and nearer the
fatal spot, until—O horror! she could not
believe her eyes—there the false cuckoo
held sweet converse with that artful minx!
The Queen was infuriated at the unbear-
able sight. Her dark eyes shot flashes,
and her suppressed voice rumbled like
distant thunder. Vatsa, indeed, looked
thunderstruck; he could neither move nor
speak. Ratnâvali had to pay the full
penalty; the Rani immediately gave orders
to have her detained in custody.

In the interests of the King, the vidûshaka did his utmost to exculpate the poor
prisoner, but Vâsavadatta was relentless.
In grateful recognition of the jester's good
services, Ratnâvali sent him, as a souvenir,
her pearl necklace of Ceylonese workman-
ship; she had saved the dainty gems from

the fatal shipwreck. The flattered recipient proudly showed the beautiful pearls to an ambassador, who had only recently arrived at King Vatsa's Court on a diplomatic errand. The foreign nobleman recognized the necklace with astonishment; long ago he had purchased it himself for his Imperial master, the Mahâ-Râja of Singhala. Princess Ratnâvali, he added mournfully, could not have worn the lovely ornament very long, for the poor girl was drowned at sea. The politic Rani, on learning that her captive was a daughter of the powerful Emperor of Ceylon, changed her tactics at once. Not only did Vâsavadatta release the fair prisoner, but she paid her marked attention and such respect as befitted the lofty station of Ratnâvali. The Queen carried her ambitious policy even so far as to offer the Princess a joint-partnership in her conjugal affections.

.   .   .   .

King Vatsa's gay amours seem to have been a favourite theme of Indian fiction during the seventh century; not unlike the more tragic love affairs of Mary Stuart, whose misfortunes furnished material to men of letters a century ago, when Scott

composed the *Abbot*, one of his finest
romances, and Schiller presented the lovely
Queen of Scots to the German stage.

PRIYADARSHIKA deals with the same subject as Ratnâvali, and was probably written
by one of King Harsha's courtiers.

The girlish voice of Priyadarshika is
heard behind the scene. When the curtain
rises, she is busy picking flowers for Vâsavadatta's supper table. The bees are buzzing
over the delicate tea roses and the fragrant
orange blossoms, and one stray wanderer
whirs about the maiden's unveiled face.
She screams out, and to King Vatsa, who
is near,

> " Her face discloses Paradise to view,
>   Eyes like a fawn's, and cheeks of rosy hue ".

To see and love beauty is one and the same
with the impressionable Râja. He chases
his troublesome rival away, and sips himself the honey off the maiden's lips, and
gently enforces her sweet confession that
one day his fondness may be requited.

A learned lady of the Queen's bed-
chamber has written a drawing-room play
entitled " The Love Story of Vatsa and
Vâsavadatta ". The performance is to

take place in the zenana.   The Rani's part
will be acted by Priyadarshika, the Râja's
by Lady Manorama, who is let into the
secret of the King's intrigue with her
fellow actress.   It has been arranged that
Manorama, in the last moment, is to send
word of her sudden indisposition and utter
inability to perform that day.   Vâsavadatta
feels annoyed that her plans are crossed,
but King Vatsa consoles her, and gener-
ously offers to take the absentee's part
himself.   Laughingly he remarks: "For
once I shall act on the stage what I am
always acting in life."   The proposal is
agreed to, and the theatricals commence.
Nature and grace impart their very best
to Priyadarshika's acting, and as to Vatsa,
he enters into the spirit of the love scenes
with undisguised zeal.   The authoress, who
sits next to Vâsavadatta, is delighted that
her comedietta should have found such
excellent interpreters.   But the Queen is
restless at the very thought that Vatsa
might carry on a flirtation with Priyadarshika, under the player's mask and licence.
And now the king-actor lifts up the lily
face of the stage-queen, and imprints kiss
after kiss on her sweet lips and eyes, and

the torrents of love passion rush in musical
Sanskrit cadence out of the secret cham-
bers of his heart. The spectators feel
transported, and encore enthusiastically.
Everyone in the distinguished audience
is in raptures except Vâsavadatta. She
hardly hears the eulogies of the spectacled
bluestocking by her side, who emphatically
declares that never in her life has she
witnessed such fine stage-acting. The
jealous Queen rises impulsively, feigning
a bad headache, and the need of fresh air.
An open gallery surrounds in a semicircle
the play-room, and is cosily furnished with
small marble tables and wicker chairs.
Palms and statuettes decorate the entrance
side, and the front overlooks the royal
gardens, which gradually lose themselves
in the distant uplands. Her Majesty
enters the gallery; she must rest a while
and calm her excited nerves. There is a
snug corner with a comfortable couch
where nobody will disturb her. But the
seat is already occupied. The vidûshaka,
who has partaken somewhat freely of the
pleasures of the table, lies on the couch
with outstretched limbs, and snores peacefully. Vâsavadatta, only too glad to vent

her ruffled temper, shakes the jester rudely;
he is sure to know when Vatsa is breeding
mischief. The poor fool rubs his drowsy
eyes in wonderment. The Queen questions him sharply, and Vatsa's confidant,
still half asleep, babbles out the whole
truth, quite unconscious of the harm he is
doing his royal master.[1]

Vâsavadatta returns at once and stops
the progress of the play. Priyadarshika is
confined to her room by the incensed
Queen, and Manorama gets a severe re-
proof. The ending of the play is similar
to that of Ratnâvali.

9. The Buddhist Theatre

In ancient India it was customary for
ruling Princes, together with their ladies
and the Court, to set out, at appointed
seasons, for a place of sacrifice up in the
vanaprastha. The royal party proceeded
to a hallowed wood, at the foot of the
Snowy Mountains where the golden soma
grew.[2] During the toilsome journey the

[1] As a rule, it is the Court fool's function, by his slashing wit,
to help his friends out of a scrape rather than lead them into
trouble.

[2] The intoxicating soma juice, to which the Indo-Iranians

Court chaplain (purohita) and his priestly staff edified the distinguished pilgrims with deva lore and the "old, old story" (purâna) of the beginning of things, and of the cosmic order. But the boisterous train of followers required coarser food, and their full allowance of fun and licence was but rarely cut short. Gleemen, in grotesque attire, their beards and faces dyed, with rattles, bells, and tambourines, danced or rather skipped along like a savage herd of giddy goats. Indeed, the hairy ajin or goatskin and the wild boar's head, emblem of a prolific stock, were quite a favourite disguise. Tokens of the fierce panther and dread lion, the kingly beasts of Shiva, and bushy tails aping the sportive monkey, added to the wanton masquerade. The revellers seemed to stroll home from a rout or riot rather than to partake in a solemn and religious act. The soul's realities and the world's

were no less partial than Europeans are to the seductive grape juice, was largely used for libations. That most potent of all charms became the soul and centre of the Vedic sacrifice. Burns has extolled John Barleycorn in song, and the ninth mandala of the Rig Veda is entirely devoted to the preparation and exaltation of King Soma. To the Âryas who quaffed the foaming soma cup, the spirit seemed divine,—adorable even above thundering Indra and blazing Agni (IX, 96[6]).

mummery, Brahma and mâya, throughout
life go hand in hand.   Every grade of
society, from the gravest to the gayest,
and from the loftiest to the grossest, was
represented in the yâtra or procession.
Gallant soldiers on whose manly brows
honour and loyalty had stamped their
mark, and beaming clerics, with a rich
vein of humour, who chuckled over a good
anecdote, or puzzled over Vedic riddles;[1]

[1] The riddles of the Rig Veda (I, 164; VIII, 29) as well as
of the kindred Edda are fragrant with the maiden bloom of
nature's poetry. "Who feeds on ashes, sleeps on stones, is
fatherless and motherless?" asks the "Old Grannie", and the
sagaman answers:

> " Fire feeds on ashes,
>   Is hid on the hearthstone,
>   Fire springs from flint."

The wolf-limbed Viking who has led the way through the
primeval wilderness, and spanned many a broad forest stream
with a floating bridge of rude oak rafts, sits in the Chieftain's timbered hall amid his boon companions, and shouts
joyfully over the brimming mead cup:

> " Pathway above us,
>   Pathway below us,
>   We went along!"

And the knowing clansmen take up the catch, and in another
snatch of song respond:

> " Birds flew above us,
>   Fish swam below us,
>   We were crossing the bridge."

Aryan paganism teems with nature riddles which are intimately
bound up with natural religion. Brahmodya, which means
"Brahma topic", is the Sanskrit word for riddle. It is a topic
which children and youthful races love,—their first crude guess
at cosmic problems.

spirited cavaliers delighting in a passage of arms, and peaceful scholars enjoying a quiet game of chess better than joust or kriegs-spiel;[1] the blue blood of the proud beauties in the chivalrous zenana, and the light-o'-love damsels of the retainers' less ceremoni-ous tents; the motley crowd of pedlars and jugglers, medicine-men and exorcists: they all came to pay homage to the gorgeous pantheon of the eye-feasting tropics. And

---

[1] A complete Indian army consisted of foot and horse (=pawns and knights), archers mounted on elephants, and warriors standing in raths or chariots. This four-limbed (chatur-anga) host, lined round the Râj and his military adviser, the Com-mander-in-chief, gave rise to the game of chatrang, which is the Indian name of chess. Like beast-fables and fairy-tales, the royal pastime came to Europe by way of islamized Persia, where King and Counsellor were renamed Shah and Vizir. The Shah's men have become our chess-men, whom the oldest Gaelic tales mention as constant companions of Irish and Highland chiefs. Christianity raised the pagan bowmen to the rank of bishops. The Vizir had to make room for the Virgin, Heaven's "Queen", to whom all roads are open. The rook is a survival of the rath, which Oriental fancy fused with the roc or simurgh,—a fabulous bird of gigantic size, able to seize elephants, and take them across the sea to the griffin's nest. Rath itself is connected with our word *ride*. The rook is also called castle, because the howdah on the tusker's back is like a movable tower that guards the tenant's exposed posi-tion. Nuptial and burial rites often preserve, at least symboli-cally, quaint customs of a ruder age. Similarly, the chessboard with kings, knights, archers, chariots, and elephants, recalls the chequered scenes of Vedic and epic warfare. In the south of London, not far from the famous inn whence the Canterbury pilgrims started, there is another tavern, the "Elephant and Castle", where chess-players used to assemble.

as the pilgrims ascended from the stifling jungle to the bracing heights, they drank wassail in soma to the azure peaks of towering Himalay lost in the watery blue. And as the panorama expanded, the awed vision of the worshippers reflected, as in the mirror of poesy, the ever-widening zone that like a coiling serpent crept round the giant waist of blue-necked Mahâdev, the mighty mountain-god whose feet are laved by Ganga. The sacrifice itself was most elaborate, and often extended over months or years. Every now and then light interludes of joyous minstrelsy relieved the monotony of weary rites and endless chants. White-locked rhapsodists, sprung from noble loins, stood up amidst their warrior kin, and the bards' melodious lips poured forth, in rhythmic cadence, the glowing panegyric of valiant sires who had earned deathless glory in the "Great Fight" (Mahâ-Bhârata) of yore. Three generations after the Battle of Kuru-kshetra, the Râja of Hastinapur, resolving to extirpate the serpent kind, instituted a Snake Sacrifice during which the thrilling incidents of the ancestral theatre of war were narrated or perhaps enacted.

Again, in a later age, another illustrious
sagaman took up each silvery thread of
the bright Kuru legend, and spun out the
fine gossamer of floating song, canto after
canto, into that thousand-coloured texture,
known as the Mahâ - Bhârata, before the
wondering sacrificers who were assembled
in Naimisha Forest.

Pâli, which was even more than Sanskrit
the language of romance and minstrelsy,
originated in Oudh, the native land of
Râma, where akkhânas, that is, tales of
the gods and national heroes, were publicly
recited on festive occasions. These old
Pâli ballads had prose and verse inter-
mixed, and were highly dramatic. They
were actually performed (as a kind of inter-
mezzo between the sacrificial acts) at the
religious gatherings of the clans, in a sacred
grove by a clear stream, or on the breezy
hilltop, first kissed by the rising sun,—in
the very presence of the pure elements as
it were. Buddhist literature, which has
preserved such akkhânas, nay, the early
Indian theatre itself, flourished in Koshala
(Oudh), where vîna-players, "drunk with
the mead of poetry",[1] had made music,

[1] Kâveyya-matta.

ever since the days of the Aryan settlement,
to the stirring folksongs which Vâlmîki
afterwards wove into the Râmâyana epic.

.   .   .   .

Strict Methodists regard it as a sin to
enter ballrooms and playhouses; and the
heretical sects of India, more particularly
the Jains and Buddhists, likewise stood up
against ballets and stage plays as tending
to demoralize human nature.[1] The canon-
ical Suttas actually forbid the faithful to
attend concerts or theatricals; but Buddhism, however strict in theory, was accom-
modating in practice, and even made use

[1] Both sects disregard the authority of the Veda, and have
separated from the Brahminic community,—the Buddhists in
the fifth century B.C., and the Jains even earlier.   Numbers
of Jains are settled in Bombay, where they occupy influential
positions as merchants and bankers. The Quakers are held
in high esteem because of their upright conduct, clean living,
and ungrudging charity. It is by the same excellent qualities
that the Jains commend themselves to their fellow countrymen.
Their very name means "victorious, triumphant" over whatever
is unrighteous and unclean. They are keen business men, extremely shrewd and cautious, and thus bear further resemblance to the Society of Friends. Very remarkable is the
extravagant kindness shown by the Jains to animals. They
are strict vegetarians, even abstaining from the use of eggs
and of unfiltered water, for fear of destroying any germ of
nascent life. Some even go so far as to take precautionary
measures in breathing, since the air teems with invisible life
quite as much as earth and water. Other Jains brush the
ground carefully before sitting down, lest they might tread
on some insect inadvertently.

of the theatre for religious propaganda. Dance and song have always been prominent features at Buddhist festivals, both sacred and profane. The fine sculpture in the Ajanta caves, with its gay and wanton scenes, bears out that fact. There is a legend of a Singhalese actress whose life was so saintly that the Holy Sangha or Synod canonized her. Dramatic spectacles in honour of the Buddha were frequently performed in Indian monasteries during the Middle Ages, and mystery plays are still given twice a year in the religious houses of Tibet. Theological controversy is mixed up with gross and farcical passages; the monks are masked as good angels, while the unclean spirits are acted by laymen.

The dramatic literature of Indian Buddhism increased fast during the centuries that intervene between the reigns of Ashoka and Harsha, but, strange to say, out of this mass of plays nothing has been preserved, apart from fragments recently discovered, save the NÂGÂNANDA or "Rejoicing of the Snakes". More than one reason can be adduced for this wholesale destruction of the Buddhist theatre. The scriptural command to keep away from playhouses implied an injunction on every good Buddhist to suppress, or at least to ignore, the drama. Moreover, the brahmins did their utmost to stunt the dangerous growth of heretic literature. And in the third place, Buddhism claimed to be the People's Religion, and naturally preferred the vulgar tongue to aristocratic Sanskrit both in the pulpit and on the stage. Its sacred books, authorized to be read in Ceylon, Burma, and Siam, are composed in Pâli, and even the later Sanskrit texts of the Indian Buddhists contain old metrical portions in a mixed dialect. The early Prâkrit theatre to which we have alluded in the second chapter must have largely consisted of Buddhist plays. King Harsha, who had a taste for letters, knew perfectly well that vernacular writings like the Jâtaka tales,[1] however popular and excellent, cannot possibly have so large a circulation as national literature. So he wisely encouraged the literary men in his capital to write Buddhist dramas in Sanskrit. Most

[1] Or, to take a more familiar example, the poetry which Burns composed in the Lowland tongue.

pieces proved worthless, and altogether
unfit to survive the season of their birth.
But one talented Court poet composed the
Nâgânanda, which pleased the gifted Râja
so much that he set the play to music himself. Such at least is the account given by
I-Tsing, a learned friar from the Far East,
who saw the Nâgânanda performed at
Kanouj, twelve hundred years ago.

Nâgas or snakes are venerated in India
as types of worldly prudence. The celestial bird Garuda, possibly a symbol of
Divine Wisdom, is fabled to have entered
a pact which entitled him to one nâga for
his daily food. Garuda is represented as
sitting on the right hand of Vishnu, and
the whole myth was perhaps intended for
a moral lesson to teach the people that
self-sacrifice is acceptable in the sight of
God.[1]

Prince Jîmûta, the hero of the Nâgânanda, once passed a mount of snake
bones, the melancholy remains of Garuda's

[1] The fabulous bird recurs in many a Buddhist legend. A
Javanese inscription of the sixth century A.D. likens the soaring
flight of wisdom to Garuda's huge wings, which spread to the
four quarters of the sky. Indian Buddhism was introduced at
an early age in Java, whence it migrated, in a corrupt form, to
the Malay Archipelago.

meals. Jîmûta felt moved to compassion, and wished to give up his body so that the poor nâga might be saved to whose pitiful lot it had fallen to be devoured that day. Garuda accepted the proffered substitute, and carried Jîmûta high up on a mountain. The flight was so rapid that a jewel dropped out of the Prince's crown, and fell upon the bronze-tinted crest of the redeemed nâga. To this day Indian snake idols display a jewel amid the clouded silver of their heads.

The Deity, well pleased with the offering, descended in a shower of amrita, which revived Jîmûta and all the nâgas that Garuda had consumed. And there was great rejoicing among the snakes over the resurrection of their dead.[1]

---

[1] Some of the Dasyus or Indian aborigines were known as Nâgas, because they dwelt in mountain caves, in the bowels of the earth, according to the Mahâ-Bhârata. Nâga tribes inhabited the highland home of King Nala, as well as the district of Nagpur, whence Princess Mâlavika took flight before the Vidarbha host. Like all primitive races, the Nâgas were fond of showy headgear and of glittering stones. Indra appears in the Rig Veda as a giant-killer and dragon-slayer; the doughty hero-god crushed the foul brood of nâgas. His feats of strength reflect the hunger for land and cattle which characterized the early Hindu invaders of the Punjab. They gradually conquered and absorbed the black-skinned natives, some of whom even contracted marriages with their Aryan rulers.

Hindu critics consider the Nâgânanda as a masterpiece of exposition, and the drama takes a high rank in Sanskrit literature.[2] The poet, in true Shakespearean fashion, has relieved the pathos of the play by some ludicrous incidents.

Shekhar is tipsy on leaving Jîmûta's

Thus, one of Arjun's wives was a Nâga Princess. The inevitable result of Aryan intermixture with coloured women were the many bastard castes which have pestered India ever since the Vedic age. Most despised of all were the degraded chandâlas, who had to make a living as butchers, grave-diggers, or executioners, being excluded from all other trades.

Garuda is akin to garut (=wing), and originally meant no more than "winged", until the magic of Aryan speech associated the word with the flame-winged lightning. During a thunderstorm, the people would say: "Now garuda cleaves jîmûta" (= the stormcloud). The deadly flashes that shoot like fiery serpents across the sky seem to consume themselves. Hence the myth arose that Garuda devours the nâgas. He came to be regarded as the archetype of the nâga-destroying or worm-eating species. Vedic sagamen depict Garuda as a huge celestial bird with gorgeous plumage, the golden-crested king of the feathered creation. And what means Jîmûta's jewelled crown but lofty cloud-rifts, sun-gilt and silver-lined? What *amrita*, food of *immortals*, but ambrosial showers, reviving and restoring the parched earth as the dread storm passes?

No doubt, the ultimate source of the Nâgânanda are historical facts interwoven with the bright fancies of Aryan nature poetry.

[2] However, the lustre which the Sanskrit drama has shed over Buddhist poetry is outshone by Pâli lyrics. Neumann's *Lieder der Mönche und Nonnen* is a spirited German rendering of a collection of fine Buddhist canticles. Some of these ecstatic outbursts of monastic song are not unworthy to take a place by the side of the mystical rhapsodies of Christian saints.

nuptial banquet. In the High Street he passes Âtreya, an old brahmin, who has the cape of his cloak wrapped over his head as a protection against the troublesome mosquitoes. Shekhar's vision is not very discriminating, and he mistakes the clean-shaven priest for his buxom sweetheart, who has promised to meet him at the corner. Shekhar falls on Âtreya's neck, kissing and hugging him, while the smell of strong drink fills unpleasantly the brahmin's nostrils. Meanwhile, the real girl appears, and seeing her lover in somebody else's embraces, she begins punching and scratching her supposed rival. At last the wench finds out her mistake, but she must needs crack another joke with that "old fool" Âtreya. She asks her young man to fetch a cup of raw brandy from the grog shop opposite, and pours the offensive liquor down the reluctant throat of the disgusted brahmin. Even then the saucy minx does not let her victim go until she has smeared sticky tamâla juice all over his plump round face.

10. Bhavabhûti

Bhavabhûti was the leading dramatist of India during the second half of the seventh century. Like Schiller he was a born idealist, his soul aglow with profound ideas of freedom and immortality. Kâlidâsa and Goethe, on the other hand, were keen observers of individual life, lovers of human nature in all its details and ramifications. It was no mere accident which led Schiller to the study of history and philosophy, Goethe to mineralogy and sculpture. Kâlidâsa was no less a realist; his poetry mirrors mankind as he saw it, and not as he wished to see it. But Bhavabhûti was a lofty moralist; his genius was logical, restless, romantic, and he was eager to leave the world better than he had found it. His father was an ecclesiastic in Berar. When the son reached early manhood, he attached himself to the then brilliant Court of Kanouj. About A.D. 700, a Kashmir army occupied Kanouj, and the victorious troops carried the prisoners of war, among them the young poet, back to their glorious Alpine home. Bhavabhûti died in Kashmir full

of years and honour. His grateful countrymen have never ceased to venerate the
sweet-voiced (shri-kantha) poet.[1]

Wallenstein, Schiller's ripest creation,
is a leaf taken from the pages of German
history, and the UTTARA RÂMA CHARITA,
Bhavabhûti's finest drama, likewise deals
with a national subject. Both plays are
preceded by introductory pieces: *Wallenstein's Lager*, in this respect, corresponds
to the MAHÂ-VÎRA CHARITA, which treats of
Râma's courtship and married life previous
to the Conquest of Lanka, while the
UTTARA RÂMA CHARITA relates events subsequent to the hero's return from Ceylon
to Koshala-land.[2]

[1] The Romans celebrated the harvest festival in honour of
Ceres, goddess of plenty. Her Indian name is Shri, who
abounds in swelling corn and ripe fruit, the sweets of Mother
Earth. Shri, as a title of distinction, is bestowed on saints,
because of the fullness and maturity of their spiritual experi-
ence, as well as on poets whose ripe genius and sweet eloquence
entitle them to homage and reverence. The giant-killer of
Koshala, far gentler than blustering Indra, is known as Shri
Râma, and Bhavabhûti as Shri-Kantha. One of the snow-
clad peaks near the sources of the Ganges, where Shiva's
meditation was undisturbed save by the sweet wild music or
the gurgling stream, is also named Shrikantha.

[2] In the field of romance, Scott's *Monastery* may be compared, though less appropriately, to the Mahâ-Vîra, and *The
Abbot* to the Uttara Râma Charita. The last word means
course, occurrence, history; vîra signifies virile, manly, heroic.
Mahâ-Vîra Charita is the Story of the Mighty Hero, i.e. of

To give a full summary of the two plays
would mean going over much of the old
ground again which we have already traversed. For the sake of completeness,
however, we will take up the thread of
Bhavabhûti's narrative where we dropped
it in telling the story of the Râmâyana.[3]

Slander was rife in the city of Ayodhya
about Râvana and Sîta. King Râma,
being more sensitive to public praise or
censure than to domestic happiness, decided to banish his faithful wife, although
he did so with a bleeding heart. In the
wilds of Dandaka Forest, poor Sîta gave
birth to Kusha and Lava, Râma's rightful
sons. The twins were brought up by Shri
Vâlmîki, the cunning saga-smith who, out
of rude folklore, fashioned the wondrous
Râmâyana epic.

The feudal barons of medieval France

Shri Râma, whose further (utter) history is told in the Uttara
Râma Charita. The Harsha Charita is a famous chronicle of
King Harsha's reign.

Charita and charya are Sanskrit participles, both akin to the
Latin "current". Brahmacharya, that is to say, the theological course or curriculum of a young brahmin, prior to his
settling down as a householder and husband, came to mean
chastity, which was enjoined on all students of divinity in
ancient India. They were to " walk (char) with Brahma" and
lead a godly life.

[3] *Short History of Indian Literature*, chapter vi.

swore allegiance on the succession of a
new sovereign, who reinstated them as
lieutenants of the Crown lands which they
held.   The Frankish kings rode round
the land in state, accepting homage and
bestowing fiefs.   They used to mount a
milk-white foal of the purest breed; its
shining mane was carefully groomed, and
adorned with sparkling jewels.   Lucky
was the man who secured a single hair
out of the sacred mane; he would treasure
it as a relic, or wear it as a charm against
misfortune.   Similar customs prevailed in
ancient India, where vassal-kings took an
oath of fealty to the Mahâ-Râja or Liege-
Lord.   At the coronation festival, or on
other solemn occasions, a young steed
(ashwa) was let loose, and a military escort followed wherever the ashwa roamed.
The tract of land thus covered was once
more declared to be subject to the Sovereign's jurisdiction.   Within the royal
demesnes, nobody was to touch the horse,
or else he ran the risk of being treated as
a rebel.   The elaborate ceremony was
called ASHWAMEDHA, because the sacrifice
of the horse terminated the proceedings.[1]

[1] Medha means sacrifice.

Râma performed an Ashwamedha, and the noble steed, being left to itself, came to Vâlmîki's hermitage. The equerries loudly proclaimed the Mahâ-Râja's suzerainty; but young Lava, resenting obeisance when it was enforced, defied the royal command, and stopped the consecrated horse, not knowing that he laid himself open to a double charge, inasmuch as he opposed paternal authority as well as the Imperial pleasure. The commander of the troop challenged the youthful offender. Lava was quite ready to break a lance with him, nay, courted the opportunity of gaining his first military laurels. Suddenly the cry arose: "Make room for the Samrâj! room for our gracious Sovereign-Lord!" It was Râma himself, clad in a tiger's skin, who entered the scene of combat, and speedily separated the gallant opponents. The Mahâ-Râja was downcast and melancholy ever since he had deserted Queen Sîta. And now he came to revisit the cherished places in the forest where he had spent his happiest years in her company.

Prince Lava, struck with admiration for the noble-looking Monarch, frankly offered

apology and homage.   Râma, too, felt
drawn to the spirited, yet gentle youth.
Kusha, who had arrived in the meantime,
looked the very image of his sire, but
neither knew the other.   The boy had
been on a visit to the sage Bharata, whose
dramatic version of the Râmâyana was to
be performed at Vâlmîki's âshram.   The
twins were to act Râma and Sîta.[1]

Bharata's play dwelt on the sufferings of
Sîta.   She attempts to end her miseries
by drowning herself in the Ganges.   But
Ganga pities and rescues her; the river
goddess appears with a new-born babe on
each arm.

Râma was so overcome with sad re-
miniscences which the play awakened in
his breast that he swooned.   The real
Sîta then came forward.   The tender and
anxious care which she bestowed on her
husband soon brought him back to consciousness, and those were blissful mo-
ments when the loving parents and their
boys were reunited and locked in a fond

[1] Indian actors (bhâratas) revere Bharata as their patron
saint.   He is an imaginary person, whose name expresses the
ancient ideals of the native stage, even as Manu is symbolic
of man's worth and aspirations, or, to come nearer home,
Britannia of Britain's Imperial mission.

embrace. The happy family returned to Ayodhya, where the repentant populace gave Sîta an enthusiastic welcome.

. . . .

The BRIHAT KATHA is a celebrated collection of old Prâkrit stories, to which the Hindus of the seventh century listened as eagerly as the Italians of the fourteenth to Boccaccio's novelettes.[1] The ocean of folklore embedded in the Brihat Katha fed the imagination of King Harsha's Court, and afforded entertainment, in an earlier age, to Kâlidâsa's contemporaries, who appreciated his magnificent setting of Shakuntala and Urvashi so keenly. But the popularity of the bright Prâkrit fables was by no means confined to India. They diffused themselves through many a literary channel in a variety of tongues, and still divert, in some recast or other, if not the drawing-rooms, at least the nurseries of Europe. The tales (akkhânas) of national heroes, narrated in the epics, and Prâkrit romance supplied Indian play-

[1] Brihat Katha means Great Narrative or Big Story-Book. The final *t* in brihat as well as bhagavat (divine) is softened before sonant letters; hence, the Sanskrit names for the Great Jungle Upanishad and the Divine Lay (India's two best religious books) are Brihad Âranyaka and Bhagavad Gîta.

wrights with ample material; Shakespeare, too, drew largely from English history and Italian fiction. VATSA'S AMOURS suggested the plot of Ratnâvali and Priyadarshika. Another favourite love story in the Katha collection bears the title MÂLATI AND MÂDHAVA, and was turned by Bhavabhûti into an original drama. The playgoers of Kanouj liked the piece so much that Uddandi, a later dramatist, changed all the names, and modernized the play. But his composition is like a Monday hash made up of the remnants of the last Sunday dinner. We will briefly examine the dramatic plot of Bhavabhûti's delightful production.

Lady Mâlati is to marry old Nandan, but although her reluctant hand is disposed of, her willing heart is secretly given to young Mâdhava. The handsome youth pursues his studies under the tuition of Kâmandaki, a learned priestess who encourages the lovers.

Mâlati and Mâdhava take a walk in the cloister gardens, and pass Nandan's sister on an ambulance. A tiger has attacked her, but Makrand, one of Mâdhava's fellow students, has killed the beast and

saved the girl. She plighted her troth
to the brave deliverer, who promised to
be true to his betrothed.

Mâdhava is in despair, and offers fervent
prayer in Kâli's temple that the goddess
may graciously avert the hapless union between Mâlati and Nandan. The black
magician who officiates at the blood-
stained shrine chants weird Tantrist and
Atharva spells, preparatory to the grue-
some slaughter of a virgin on the sacrificial altar. Mâdhava hears distinctly the
piteous cries of the secreted victim. Surely
he knows that voice, and rushes to her
rescue. It is Mâlati, whom he snatches
from the bloodthirsty clutches of the mad
fanatic.

Kâmandaki bids the lovers take courage
when the dread marriage morning dawns.
She will steer them safely through every
difficulty. Indeed, prudence and daring
are wonderfully blended in the fine character of Kâmandaki. At her suggestion,
Nandan's young bride is to be attired in
festive garb at the very convent over which
the shrewd priestess presides. She then
arranges a secret meeting between Mâlati
and Mâdhava in the dormitory, and marries

them according to Buddhist rites. The young pair leave unobserved, and in order that they may gain time, Makrand dons Mâlati's wedding gown.

The disguised student is taken in solemn procession to Nandan's house, where he goes through the prescribed marriage ceremony. At last the supreme moment comes when the eager bridegroom is left alone with his young wife. As with a trembling hand he raises the nuptial veil, Nandan receives a kick so violent that his limbs ache and his eyes water. The startled courtier, groaning and sighing, hobbles out of the room, and his pretty sister has to listen to a mournful tale. She volunteers to mediate and speak to her unmannerly and rather masculine sister-in-law. On entering the bridal chamber, she finds herself in the virile arms of her fond lover. After a hurried explanation, Makrand elopes with his lady fair. The two join Mâlati and Mâdhava in their place of retreat.

The romantic flight of the runaway couples being discovered, Nandan, with the King's sanction, has a patrol of soldiers sent after the fugitives. Makrand and Mâdhava repulse the pursuers and come

victorious out of the skirmish. Their
spirited and successful resistance secure
them the royal favour, and a double wedding
feast is celebrated with great pomp, and is
honoured by the Râja's presence, poor old
Nandan acting as best man to Makrand.[1]

11. The National Drama

In the age of silver, Vishnu came down
from heaven for the sixth time to lead
suffering humanity once more from sin and
error unto salvation. At that time, the
orthodox brahmins were in danger of being
superseded by the rationalistic warrior caste.
In order to suppress heresy and scepticism,
Vishnu became incarnate as Parashu-Râma
or "Râma with the Axe", who is altogether
a different personality from Râma, the
saintly King of Oudh. Thrice seven times
Râma with the Axe subdued the kshatriyas,
and made the priestly caste the paramount
power in India. Native art represents the
avatâr as a giant of colossal size and strength

[1] Makrand is short for Makaranda. Nandan must neither
be confounded with Nanda, the foster-father of Krishna, nor
with Ânanda, one of Buddha's disciples. Mâdhava, too, has
to be kept distinct from his namesake, the Râja of Nagpur (in
Kâlidâsa's play).

wielding a mighty battleaxe.[1]   One day he walked along the cliffs of the Malabar coast, when the ocean-god growled at him and tried to impede his progress.   Parashu-Râma then struck his axe deep in the solid rock.   Wide clefts and inlets were formed by the force of the blow, and Father Ocean rushed into the trap, foaming and howling, while the avatâr pursued his way quietly.

Another legend accounts differently for the creeks and firths which indent the rocky coast of South-western India.   Hanuman, commander-in-chief of the vânar (monkey) army, whose fights with the demons of Ceylon are narrated in the Râmâyana, was endowed with literary as well as military skill.   He turned Vâlmîki's epic into a national play, and scratched the soft Sanskrit verses which he had composed into the hard sandstone of the Western Ghats. Vâlmîki felt uneasy lest the excellence of the new drama might injure the well-established fame of the heroic poem.   The good-natured monkey-general then tore the

---

[1] The pelican, a water bird, whose beak is somewhat shaped like a pickaxe, is named after the Greek word peleku, which both in sound and meaning agrees with the Sanskrit parashu (axe).   Avatâr signifies descent, a visible incarnation of the Deity.

impress off the huge mountain crags, and
cast it in the sea.   Part of the rock-typed
script was accidentally recovered by some
Indian sailors in the eleventh century, when
Bhoja was king.   The cultured Râja entrusted Dâmodar, his poet-laureate, with
the arduous task of joining and recasting
the bulky fragments for the Malva stage.
Though being an abridgment, Dâmodar's
play sadly lacks brevity.   Its fourteen acts
possess antiquarian interest rather than literary value.[1]

.   .   .   .

Bhatta Nârâyan, who lived a hundred

[1] In the age of the Râmâyana, fierce tribes of aborigines
roamed through the Dekhan woodlands.   It was a common
sight for Aryan settlers from the north to see the wild men
of the wood suddenly burst from the mountain caves in which
they slept, and quench their thirst at a river's brink, or climb
the majestic vanaspatis, i.e. jungle-lords, to pick the edible
fruit off the laden branches.   Hence the jungle-roving bands
of savage monkeys and uncouth natives were both called
vânars or foresters;   the word is derived from vana (forest).

Hanumat, or Hanuman as he is generally styled in Europe,
is one of the most popular figures in Eastern folklore.   There
is a Malay tradition that the venturous leader of the vânar
host, after the Conquest of Lanka (Ceylon), dwelled in Java,

> "Living on fruit and nuts, and dressed
> In coat of bark and deerskin vest",

the customary garb of Indian ascetics.   Even now the Javanese
make regular pilgrimages to the vanaprastha where the volun-
tary exile is believed to have done penance, in order that he
might gain heaven.

years after Bhavabhûti, made Draupadi
the heroine of a national drama. After
the fatal game of dice,[1] the Kaurava
brothers looked upon Draupadi as their
rightful property. When she objected to
be treated as a slave, one of them dragged
the Princess by her beautiful thick hair
across the spacious banquet hall. Bhîma,
trembling with rage, re-bound her dishev-
elled tresses, and swore to avenge the
disgrace. Many years after, on the battlefield of Kurukshetra, he made good the
oath, and slew his insolent cousin.

Bhatta Nârâyan has drawn the various
characters of the Mahâ-Bhârata very graph-
ically. Vindictive Bhîma and imperious
Karna stand out in bold contrast to well-
balanced Arjun. Duryodhan, in his own
estimation, shows much foresight and dignity, although, in reality, he is pig-headed
and overbearing. Yudhishthir acts like a
true gentleman: courteous, gallant, true
to his word, and ever ready to sacrifice
his private interests to the common good.

But the fierce Mahâ-Bhârata was, at no
time, so popular on the Indian stage as
the gentler sister-epic. The Hindus never

---

[1] *Short History of Indian Literature*, chapter iv.

seem to tire of a story told of the saintly
Râma. The Nepalese theatre in the north
is known to have produced Râma plays as
early as the fourteenth century of our era.
The Tamil theatre in the south has shown
itself no less partial to the Râmâyana.[1] The
dramatic literature of India does not stand
alone in the tendency to revert to national
subjects. The theme of many a Greek
tragedy is taken from the *Iliad*, and various
German poets have composed Nibelung
plays. *Cid Campeador* has found favour
on the Spanish stage, and *King Arthur* was
received with enthusiasm by large London
audiences. Hosts of Indian dramas are
derived from the Râmâyana. Some of
them lay the scene in the royal palace at
Mithila, others outside the city gates of
Lanka, others again in the glades of Dandaka Forest. One author introduces a
house party of Shakuntala's father, a power-

[1] Nepalese belongs to the Sanskrit stock of languages; musical Tamil is a Dravidian or Indo-Turanian tongue. Chinese
and Tamil are the only Turanian languages that have produced
dramas of any value.

The Javanese, too, have fondly preserved the memory of
Râma, but they are more attached to the heroes of the "Great
Epic". The Mahâ-Bhârata, which is extant in a Kavi version,
lingers on in many legends and place names throughout the
Isle of Java.

ful rishi who is about to perform an elaborate sacrifice in his forest bungalow. Among Vishwâmitra's invited guests are King Janaka and his daughter Sîta, the sage Gautama and his wife Ahalya, Prince Râma and his brother Lakshman. Râma and Sîta meet for the first time. Indra is also present, but the god has rendered himself invisible because he feels ashamed of being seen committing adultery with the beautiful Ahalya. But Gautama, by virtue of his holiness, detects the hideous crime, and is so incensed at the foul deed that he transforms his wife into a dangerous cliff, as a warning to others that she cannot be trusted.

By far the most spirited Râma play is a comedy of errors written by Râmabhadra. The poet, who resided in the Dekhan, was a contemporary of the author of *Tartuffe*. Sîta's swayamvara[1] gives rise to some scenes of exquisite humour. Her suitors try to bend an unwieldy bow, Râma alone succeeds. Parashu-Râma is one of the unsuccessful rivals. Regarding every kshatriya as a born enemy of the human race,

---

[1] The ceremony of choosing a husband is described in the *Short History of Indian Literature*, chapter iv.

the avatâr challenges Râma to single combat, but is defeated and, at the same time,
reconciled to the generous victor. A far
more dangerous opponent than bluff and
honest Parashu-Râma is the treacherous
Râvana. Spiteful because Sîta has rejected
his suit, and hating Râma because she has
accepted him, the Râkshasa King requests
the conquered hero to lend him his parashu
or battleaxe, so that he might slay the
troublesome Kshatriya Prince. When the
petition is scornfully declined, Râvana se-
cures his sister's co-operation. The Râkshasa Princess metamorphoses herself into
Sîta's likeness, and is to stab the Koshala
Prince with a poisoned dagger. Râvana's
butler is disguised as Râma, and has orders
to lure Sîta away from her friends. Princess
and butler travel by different routes, but
happen to arrive at their destination simul-
taneously. They are got up so excellently
that they mistake each other for Râma and
Sîta, and are caught in their own trap.
The real objects of their evil design, unnoticed by the deceived deceivers, are not
far off, and feel somewhat alarmed when
they behold their exact counterfeits. The
two pretenders, evasive and inquisitive

alike, become so enamoured of one another, as they carry out the diplomatic part of their errand, that they forget all about murder and abduction. Intoxicated with tender glances and fervent kisses, both messengers break faith to the demon-king, and, taking each other into their confidence, disclose every detail of their criminal intention. Only slowly the humiliating truth dawns on the clumsy pair of rogues: they are dealing with the wrong party, and have made fools of themselves! After reconsidering their position, the impostors decide to do Râvana's commission after all. But Râma has heard quite enough of the unclean colloquy to be convinced of their guilt. He kills the butler and wounds the Princess. She takes flight to Ceylon. Her brother is furious that she has been duped, and devises another plot.

In the next act, Râma is seen hunting in a well-stocked wood, when Sîta's image is suddenly conjured up before his enchanted vision. It is a trick due to Râvana's jugglery. The loving husband points out the luring image to his Court jester, who cannot see the mirage, and rightly suspects black râkshasa magic. Two Lanka emis-

saries, transformed into the semblance of
Râma's jester, and Vishwâmitra's scribe,
then enter the stage. They are to detain
Râma until Râvana has decoyed the real
Sîta. The unforeseen presence of the true
jester comes as an unpleasant surprise, but
the quick-witted sham-scribe whispers in
Râma's ear: "Be on your guard, Sire, for
that fool by your side is not your vidûshaka,
but a râkshasa in disguise." Râma is deaf
to the address of either friend or foe, and
only sees Sîta's illusive form. In the meantime, the sham-fool, who has sufficient wit
to keep in the background, is joined by the
real scribe, and both, in their turn, are
mistaken as regards each other's identity.
After some more blunders on either side,
and many a comic situation arising there-
from, all four are confronted in the end,
and the whole fraud is exposed. The
genuine scribe and jester now implore
Râma earnestly to return with them at
once, but the two tricksters put the Prince
into a deep trance, and suggest to his impressionable mind that Sîta is distracted at
the thought of his prolonged absence, and
in her despair means to throw herself down
yon precipice. Poor Râma, ruler of multi-

tudes, is no longer master of himself.   In
his subconscious state he feels an exquisite
pain at the intimation of the horrible news,
and hurries after the imaginary Sîta, being
determined either to save his love or to share
her untimely death.   The jugglers are jubilant, but a miracle is wrought by the grace
of Heaven, and puts them to confusion.
The cliff which the deluded visionary as-
cends, shrinks of a sudden and contracts to
a woman's form.   It is Dame Ahalya, to
whom the sanctifying touch of the pure-
souled Râma has given back her human
shape.   By Indra's help, she is able to
show her gratitude and take the hypnotic
spell off her deliverer.   The two demons,
seeing the day go against them, presently
change into a pair of swift-footed antelopes,
and skip off hurriedly in different directions.
Râma goes in search of Sîta, and is only
just in time to rescue her from the brutal
force of Râvana.   At the husband's unexpected sight, the vile demon-king lets
go his prey and takes to shameful flight.

Râma literature has, in proportion to the
population, even a larger circulation in
Ceylon than on the continent of India.   As
the Singhalese are passionately fond of

music and dancing, Râma and Sîta have
been transferred from the national theatre
to the operatic stage, just as Sigfrid and
Brunhild, in Germany, have passed from
the theatrical boards to the opera house.
Râma operas are much appreciated in
Kandy and Colombo, and often last from
sunset until dawn, some of them being half
as long as Wagner's *Ring*.

12. Râjashekhar

Nâtaka is the technical term for a Hindu
drama in which doughty knights and high-
born damsels utter lofty thoughts, and display noble sentiments. Nâtikas, on the
other hand, touch on domestic incidents
such as occur among the humbler classes.[1]
Hamlet and *King Lear* come under the
former heading, *The Merry Wives of
Windsor* and *She Stoops to Conquer*
under the latter. The heroic comedies of
Spain, in which royalty, priestly mages,
and national heroes are staged, resemble
the Hindu nâtakas, but the *comedias de*

[1] These definitions are laid down in Bharata's dramaturgy,
which native tradition derives from the Nâtya Veda or ancient
Stage Wisdom.

capa y espada, with their gay *personnel* of private cavaliers wearing "cape and sword" after the Spanish fashion, and attended by blustering serving-men, are more like nâtikas. Again, in the kindred branch of fiction, Scott's romances might well be compared to nâtakas, because the leading characters are, as a rule, of noble birth, and speak choice English,—the homely Lowland dialect (broad Scotch) being employed by minor figures only. But Dickens's novels would be nâtikas, since they move on a lower social plane, and introduce a jumble of Cockney English and provincial slang. The leading personages in a Hindu nâtaka converse in polished Sanskrit. Nâtikas, on the other hand, have a much larger admixture of Prâkrit dialogue. A nâtika written entirely in Prâkrit is called sattaka. Most sattakas are spectacular pieces, full of the sensational and the marvellous, but deficient in psychological interest. Numbers of them were penned in the old literary vernaculars, such as Mahârâshtri and Shauraseni, but only one, composed by Râjashekhar, has survived. The poet, who appears to have lived in the tenth century of our era, has also left a nâtaka, which we will briefly examine as an illustration of his dramatic talent.

The soothsayers have predicted that whosoever marries Lady Âvali shall gain overlordship of India. Vidyâdhar's Prime Minister firmly believes in the truth of the oracle, and intends to make the damsel one of the Râja's wives. In order to carry out the patriotic scheme, he induces Âvali's father, who is Governor of a remote province, to have his daughter presented at Court. The loyal minister and his wife invite the young lady to spend a season at their town house. One day the King calls, and their pretty guest is given an opportunity to see Vidyâdhar without being seen by him. The consequence is that Âvali falls in love with the handsome Râja. The Premier's wife, in whom she confides, easily persuades her fair visitor to don boy's clothes, and enter the royal household as a page. As Âvali bears a striking resemblance to her younger brother Varma, there is but little difficulty in introducing her at the palace by his name.

In the next act, the Râja makes love to Princess Kuvalay, the daughter of a vassal king, without heeding the pitiful remonstrances of his indignant spouse, who is resolved to pay the insult back with interest. The Queen makes Vidyâdhar believe that young Varma, with her permission, has sent for his sister, the boy feeling lonely without the accustomed playmate. The artful Rani, well knowing the King's amorous disposition, even throws out an ironical hint that on her part there would be no serious objection to his marriage with Lady Âvali, whom she represents as good-looking and accomplished. Her Majesty's real intention is to have the beardless page dressed up as Âvali, and after the Râja's mock wedding with the youth, to celebrate Varma's nuptials with Kuvalay. By this clever stratagem she means to kill two birds with one stone; to dispose of a troublesome rival, and to humiliate the King.

Vidyâdhar, after consulting his Prime Minister, readily agrees to the treacherous proposal, all the more eagerly as he is delighted with Âvali's portrait, which he has seen in the Premier's house. By royal command the apparent Varma is robed in bridal garments, and all the maids-of-honour laughingly declare that the lad looks, to perfection, every inch a girl—as is really the case. Kuvalay loves the Râja dearly, and willingly consents to be one of the bridesmaids, upon the Queen's word of honour that the Princess, too, is to marry the King directly after his wedding with Lady Âvali.

The nuptial rites are nearly completed when a mounted courier brings a private message from Âvali's noble parent, thanking the Queen for the gracious reception she has been pleased to give his daughter at the zenana, and entreating Her Majesty to make the measure of her kindness full by finding a suitable husband for the motherless girl. The Rani is hopelessly entangled in her own meshes, and unable to retract a marriage which has been solemnized at her bidding. Nor can she honourably refuse the redemption of her pledge to Kuvalay, whose legal union with the King must now receive her sanction. The Queen, indeed, is wise in her folly. With the best possible grace she begs the Râja to accept two brides at her hands. She makes light of her deep-laid schemes, and greets both ladies smilingly as her

dear sisters and junior partners in the
affections of her lord. Official despatches
convey the welcome intelligence that the
royal arms have been victorious east and
west, and that Vidyâdhar is acknowledged
as Samrâj or Universal Emperor of Hindustan. The play ends with his proclamation
as Kaisar-i-Hind.[1]

Râjashekhar was not only a prolific

[1] In the Heroic Age Indian ladies held a higher place than
with advancing culture. Epic India can boast of a Nala and
Râma; like Hector and Ulysses, the two râjas contracted
one marriage only. But even Sîta was banished by her husband, while Damayanti and Shakuntala were cruelly deserted.
Polytheism has lured many a contemplative pagan into panthe-
istic visions which tend to destroy the healthy sense of personality and moral responsibility. In like manner, polygamy,
which has long been the general system among the Hindu
aristocracy, is fatal to conjugal fidelity and to domestic peace.
Western civilization at least professes purer ideals; the laws of
Europe punish bigamy as a grave offence. The sanctity of
Christian wedlock is but a perpetuation of the dignity and
respect enjoyed by Roman matrons. The countrymen of
Lucretia and Virginia had only one lawful wife, and the domi-
nance of monogamy in Romance and Teutonic countries may
well be due, as Lecky points out, to the expansion of Roman
rule.

We have considerably altered the story of Râjashekhar's
play to suit the purpose of this book. The names, too, have
been shortened. In the original, Râja and Princess are called
Vidyâdharamalla and Kuvalayamâla, while sister and brother
bear the formidable names Mrigânkâvali and Mrigânkavarman.
Kuvalaya, which signifies "water lily", may be conveniently
pronounced Kuvalay, after the precedent of Himalay. The
poet's name must be kept distinct from Shekhar, one of the
dramatis personæ in the Nâgânanda.

writer, but an expert penman familiar with
the technique of stage effects. But there
is a lack of individuality in many of his
characters. The poet has also contributed
to the National Theatre of India. His
LITTLE RÂMÂYANA is about twice the
length of *King Henry the Eighth*. All
that is preserved of the LITTLE MAHÂ-
BHÂRATA is a fragment consisting of two
acts; death seems to have intervened before the drama could be completed. The
LITTLE RÂMÂYANA deserves brief mention.
Sîta is forcibly detained by Râvana, who
flies into a passion because she scorns to
listen to his insolent suit. He then gives
way to a melancholy mood. The Lord
Chamberlain of Lanka is much concerned
about his brooding master, and feels duty-
bound to cheer him up. Having an inventive turn of mind, his lordship con-
structs a huge doll which somewhat resembles Sîta. The large eyeballs roll
from side to side, and the ruby lips are
slightly parted. A parrot, trained to talk
certain words of affection, is placed inside
the doll's head. The demon-king laughs
heartily at the comical effect, and feels all
the better for the clever entertainment. A

good laugh is often better than the best sermon.

13. Marionettes and Pantomimes

The large cities of India have proper theatres, both stationary and itinerant, just as London, New York, or Melbourne, but the teeming millions up and down the country are deprived of the pleasure and instruction which stage-acting is intended to confer. The only kind of spectacle accessible to the Indian peasantry, more particularly in the Dekhan, are puppet shows set up in the open fields or on the highroad. The Sanskrit for actor is mâgadha or bhârata; the word for puppet is panchâli. It is obvious that the Gangetic valley, which gave birth to epic minstrelsy, is also the home of Indian theatricals. Travelling shows may have originated in Panchâla-land, and spread over the Dekhan, and thence across the sea to the Malay Archipelago. Panchâli entertainments are known to have been popular in ancient Java. Europe is not without a parallel. Punch and Judy migrated from the South of Italy, their native

land, through France to the British Isles.[1]
The oldest Indo-European book in
which puppets are mentioned is the Mahâ-
Bhârata. The Brihat Katha alludes to a
young girl who amuses herself with a set
of movable dolls. One of them can dance,
by means of some mechanical contrivance,
another screeches, and a third carries a
tiny cup of water without spilling it.—It
is the custom of Indian showmen to pro-
ceed on a local tour after exhibiting in the
busy thoroughfares of Madras, Bombay,
and other towns. Horns are blown, and
gongs are beaten, in order to attract public
attention. The puppets are made of wood
and cardboard, and can be easily worked
with strings or by wire.[2] Their limbs are
cleverly jointed so that the panchâlis may

---

[1] "Punch" has nothing whatever to do with panchâli or with
punching people's heads, but is a contraction of Punchinello
or rather Pulcinello, the buffoon of the Neapolitan stage. The
Italian word is connected with "pullet", and means chicken-
hearted, with reference to Mr. Punch's empty bragging and
boasting. Subsequently, popular fancy associated Punch with
Pontius Pilate, and mated him with Judy, i.e. Judas. The five-
fold mixture of brandy and hot water to which lemon, spice, and
sugar are added is also called punch, which, like the Panchâlas
or Five Boroughs, is derived from pancha, the Sanskrit word
for five.

[2] The high antiquity of Indian puppet shows is corroborated
by the term sûtra-dhâra, i.e. stage manager. The word means
literally "holding the strings, pulling the wires".

freely gesticulate with arms and legs. The programme of the travelling troupes generally contains a large variety of items. The movements of the gaudily dressed dummies are adapted to the recital of a light and laughable dialogue. As a rule, the subject is taken from the traditional lore of the two national epics. But political history has considerably enlarged the repertoire. Stories of Alexander's invasion, incidents from the fierce fights with Hun and Moslem, the English Conquest, and the Indian Mutiny mark some of the stages in the evolution of the Hindu puppet show. Punch and Judy have grown up under similar conditions. The early shows in England were strictly confined to religious subjects. The Virgin Mary and the blessed saints were the principal marionettes previous to the Reformation; the building of Solomon's Temple, Jonah and the whale, and other Biblical stories furnished additional entertainment.[1]   But pro-

[1] The marionettes of the old Italian exhibitions were originally, as the name imports, miniature images of the Virgin Mary. The Punch and Judy show has long been divested of its sacred character, but is still termed Marionette Theatre in Continental countries. Wax figures of the Blessed Virgin used to be carried in Roman Catholic processions, and it is here that the historical origin of the European panchâlis must be looked for.

fane history came to be associated with
the marionette stage in the stirring age
of Queen Elizabeth, and gradually superseded sacred subjects.   The battles with
the Spaniards, and the destruction of the
Armada, Drake and Raleigh, gold-digging
in Peru, and tobacco-planting in Virginia,
were the talk everywhere in merry England, at Court and on 'Change, in the
coffee taverns in Fleet Street, and at the
puppet shows on Holborn Bridge.   No
less popular were the marionette theatres
on the other side of the Channel.   Goethe
narrates in *Wilhelm Meister* (translated by
Carlyle) how interested his countrymen
were in them, and to what excellence
marionette exhibitions developed in Germany during the eighteenth century.   After
the Battle of the Nile, Nelson became a
favourite with the English, his deeds being
celebrated in music halls and on the puppet
boards. "Punch, my boy!" the naval hero
is reported to have said on one occasion,
"come on board my good ship, and help
me to fight the French. I'll make you a
captain or a commodore, if you like it."

   "But I don't like it," whimpered Mr.
Punch, "I might get drowned."

"Never fear that," retorted Nelson; "he who is born to be hanged is sure not to be drowned."

The people of India look upon dumb-shows with as much favour as the English do on Christmas pantomimes. Bishop Heber describes the "Siege of Lanka" as he saw it performed at the Râm-Lîla festival in Allahabad: Râvana's palace was constructed of bamboo reeds, and decorated with coloured paper. Doors and windows were gaily painted, and a frightful paper giant stood on the roof of the building. The ogre was fifteen feet high, and had twelve arms, with some kind of weapon in each. At his feet sat a little girl meant to be Sîta; two green dragons made of inflated bladder were guarding the prisoner. The poor little mite was wrapped in a gorgeous veil, and must have felt very tired, for she drooped her curly head, and was soon fast asleep. Hanuman, having a monkey's mask pulled over his ears, was capering and gambolling outside the city gates. He had a long bushy tail, and his skin was dyed with indigo. Two strapping lads, about twelve years of age, represented Râma and Lakshman. They were holding levee under a spacious awning, and each carried a toy sabre in his right hand and a gilt bow in his left. All sorts of trinkets covered their slim bodies, the bare parts being daubed with chalk and vermilion. Large crowds of spectators almost blocked the road, and the pageant lasted three consecutive nights. [1]

[1] In England the rites of May were observed with games, sports, masques, and dances. The great sight at a Mayfair was the mock fight between the black winter giant and the white-horsed knight, who was to snatch Maid Marian, the Queen of Sunshine, out of the ogre's open jaws. The final scene was a gleaming sword dance, in which the giant-killer once more displayed his swordcraft. The fiddlers played a lively jig; the hobby horse, profusely decked with sprigs of may and bunting, pranced gaily as in a courtly tilt; romantic lore, glee, jest, satire were freely scattered in a jumble of song. Meddlesome hawkers sold the latest ballad of the dragon-slayer's doughty deeds, and how the king's daughter was set free from the cloud-giant's gloomy dungeon. The old guy of a dragon, a clumsy piece of carpentry and mummery, was burnt in a crackling bonfire, amidst shouts of jollity, and Maid Marian was crowned Queen of the May.

Puppet show and sword dance have come down from hoary antiquity, and were associated with unclean pagan rites. The early Church recast and renamed both Marionettes and Mary's or Morris dancers. The gallant fight of sportive Spring and crabbed Winter has ever been a favourite topic of

14. Politics on the Stage

Among the most precious gems in the casket of English literature are Shakespeare's historical plays. His immortal brush has touched up and given lustre to three hundred years of English warfare and kingship. But the history of India has been sadly neglected by her great poets. Only two Sanskrit dramas record a brief span of political events: MÂLAVIKA AND AGNIMITRA by Kâlidâsa, and the MUDRA-RÂKSHASA by Vishâkhadatta. The former play is rich in poetic sentiment, and glows with the fire of a warm imagination. The characteristic points of the Mudra-Râkshasa, on the other hand, are a dry humour, and that cold glitter which, now

Aryan nature poetry. The reverse of our gold coins still commemorates "St. George and the Dragon", and the knight's cream-coloured charger (the golden sunbeams) lingers on, though a mere shadow, in the "gee-gees", with tinkling bells and gaudy trappings, at the merry-go-round of country fairs. But the real significance of the dragon fight (the triumph of light over darkness) has been forgotten, and the oldest English folk dance, which reflects the annual spring drama, is often explained away as a Moorish (= Morris) or Spanish custom.

and again, renders the budget speech of
some great parliamentarian so brilliant and
effective.   According to native scholars,
Vishâkhadatta was a younger contemporary of Bhavabhûti, but it is tempting to
reflect that he might have lived towards
the end of the twelfth century, when the
Mohammedan armies had nearly completed
the conquest of Hindustan.   In that case,
it must have been with a sigh of regret
and a sense of relief that the poet's
musing mind turned from the national
humiliation back to the distant time of
Alexander's departure from India, and to
the subsequent consolidation of the vast
Hindu colossus under the vigorous rule of
Chandragupta.

That great Emperor reposed full confidence in Chânakya, his Imperial Chancellor, who is represented as having slain
King Nanda, and helped Chandragupta to
mount the throne of Magadha.   The new
ruler, who had sprung from lowly ranks,
found more favour with the people than
with the nobles of Magadha;   he was
particularly odious to Lord Râkshasa,
the trusty old minister of Nanda.[1]   The

[1] Râkshasa must not be associated with his mythical name-

honourable statesman denounced and repudiated the unscrupulous usurper; but
swimming against the popular current, he
was in constant danger of his life. At
length, Râkshasa fled from Patna under
cover of night. Owing to his influence
and rectitude, he was soon able to form
a powerful coalition among the neighbour-
ing Râjas against the royal upstart.

Chânakya was at once crafty in his
dealings and loyal to his master. It was
the aim of his policy to strengthen the
government in power by means of estrang-
ing Râkshasa from the confederate Princes,
and, if possible, of winning him over to
Chandragupta's side. To gain that end,
the Chancellor deliberately provoked the
Emperor's displeasure, and then suddenly
withdrew from the royal presence, appar-
ently in deep resentment.

In the meantime, the ex-minister was
busy organizing the opposition. Chânakya's
spies followed him everywhere, and watched
his movements as closely as their personal
safety would permit. They had instruc-

sakes, the savage Râkshasas of primitive Ceylon, nor King
Nanda with Krishna's foster-father. Nanda or Ânanda means
Joy, like our Letitia, but is a man's name. Mâlati's jilted
fiancé is Nandan.

tions to spread the false rumour that Chandragupta had bribed Râkshasa, who was
playing a double game. They even inti-
mated that he had been offered the post
of Chânakya, who had forfeited the Imperial favour on account of his overbearing and dictatorial measures. At first the
alarmist report was hardly taken seriously.
But it was believed more readily when
some commercial travellers returned from
Magadha with the sensational news that
the great Chancellor was actually in disgrace with the Emperor. The Râja at
whose Court Râkshasa was staying at the
time could not help suspecting his guest
of treachery, but as there was not sufficient
evidence to prove his guilt, he was simply
given notice to quit the State at once.

Râkshasa, disguised as a pedlar, returned
to Patna, where he rejoined his wife and
children; he had left them under the care
of a dear old friend, a goldsmith by trade.
No sooner was Chânakya apprised of Râkshasa's secret arrival than he threw his
cards down openly, and showed his hand
to Chandragupta, who not only pardoned
the Chancellor's shrewd audacity, but was
delighted with the bold stroke of policy.

A warrant was issued for Râkshasa's arrest, and a charge of high treason was brought against the jeweller for harbouring a political spy. Râkshasa was taken before Chânakya, who left him the alternative either to become the cause of his friend's ignominious death, or to prove himself not to be a spy and sedition-monger, but a supporter of the present government. "And the best way Your Excellency can do that," Chânakya added blandly, "is to accept a ministerial post which His Majesty is pleased to offer you through me." Râkshasa was touched by the Chancellor's delicate advances, and entered Chandragupta's service.[1]

15. A Metaphysical Play

Vedânta has left traces everywhere on the popular cults of India, however much they merged gnâna into bhakti—self-identification with the Infinite into adoration

[1] The plot of the Mudra-Râkshasa resembles the dramatic crisis of Shakuntala in so far as both plays are built up around a mudra or signet-ring. Wilson's *Theatre of the Hindus* (2 vols., 3rd edition, London, 1871) contains readable translations of the more important dramas discussed in chapters vi, vii, viii, x, and xiv.

of a personal Redeemer. Early Christian influences have intensified the element of bhakti in Krishnaism, and still more in Râmaism. But even Tulsi Das (+1624), who sang a new song of Râma, the friend of sinners, could not have composed his fervent bhakti poetry, that treasury of Hindu devotion, without a conception of Vedânta.[1]

Krishnamishra, who flourished in the beginning of the twelfth century, wrote a play to the glory of Vedânta. The title is PRABODHA CHANDRODAY, or the Rise of the Moon of True Knowledge.[2] Hundreds of years before Bunyan thought of personifying Christian virtues and vices, Krishnamishra composed this Indian pilgrim's progress in a dramatic form. To convey the spirit of the Prabodha Chandroday adequately, we have ventured on a paraphrase, rendering the quaint Sanskrit terminology in the more familiar garb of Western thought.

Truth and Error are the sons of Individual Consciousness, and grandsons of

---

[1] The Vedânta philosophy is explained in the *Short History*, chapter ix.

[2] As Himalay is short for Himâlaya, so Chandroday for Chandrodaya, which, again, is a contraction of Chandra-udaya, i.e. the moon's rising.

King Infinite.   The children of Truth are Faith and Reason, their respective issue being Religion and Science.   Error begets a long line of descendants, who gradually take possession of the earth.

Error is the first to appear on the stage. He remarks to his Prime Minister what a good thing it is that the dominion of Truth is dwindling every day.   He is only troubled about an old prophecy that Prince Vedânta is to be born from the spiritual contact of Science and Religion, and that Vedânta is destined to destroy Error.   Such an event, the minister observes, is happily far off, because the two cousins have long been divorced, and every attempt to bring them together again has hitherto been vain.

The next actor to come forward is King Truth.   On seeing the white-robed Râja with his shining crown, Error hastily beats his retreat.   Truth is presently joined by his wife, Queen Love, who bears the joyful tidings that she has reconciled Science and Religion after all.

The situation looks grave for the party in opposition, and King Error hurriedly summons a Cabinet Council.   The heir to the throne, Prince I-Come-First, attends,

so does the Premier, and all the other
ministers of Error. The Rev. Dr. Cocksure, expounder of the latest theology
which is established in the land of Error,
urges the honourable members of the
Council to capture Benares, and deliver
the holy city out of the enemy's hands.
"Whoever holds Benares", are the closing
words of his eloquent oratory, "possesses
the key of India. I pray God to help us
in this most righteous enterprise against
the vile pretender who goes by the name of
Truth Revealed." A resolution is passed
unanimously; Error's forces are to take
the sacred city by storm.

After a long siege Benares surrenders.
The townsmen forswear Truth, and sub-
mit to the rule of Error. The new King
grants an audience to General Chârvâka,
who typifies the materialistic school of
Hindu thought.[1] Chârvâka reports that
a mutiny has broken out in Bengal and
Orissa, and that the insurgents have resolved henceforth to throw in their lot
with the forlorn cause of Truth. This
outrageous rebellion is believed to be due
to the secret workings of Queen Love.

[1] Chârvâka means literally "glib talker".

The incensed general receives orders to mobilize King Error's well - disciplined troops at once; they are to attack Truth, and oppose Love's machinations.

The next act introduces a gentle, timid girl who is dead-tired, and piteously cries for her mother. The maiden's name is Devotion; she is the favourite daughter of Princess Faith. Buddhism, Jainism, and other heretic upstarts crowd the stage with their ostentatious wives. All these ladies pose as Faith. Devotion cheers up on hearing her dear mother's name, but when she beholds the showy and ugly persons who have assumed it, her tears flow copiously. The various "isms" console her with high-flown ethics and metaphysics, but their verbosity is cut short by the appearance of General Chârvâka. The gallant soldier is attended by a smart *corps-de-ballet*, and, in his turn, enlivens the dull lecturers with utilitarian principles. Everyone present, be he Vedic believer or Noncon-formist, must pledge him with a cup of wine and tread a gay measure. Chârvâka asks sweet Devotion for the first dance, and informs his fair partner where Faith is to be found. "All these so-called faiths are humbugs," he remarks; "there is but one true faith, my dear, and that is—'Eat, drink, and be merry'."

Chârvâka, not satisfied with ridiculing Faith, insults her personally, but Love, who can do all things, shields her friend, and sends the following message to King Truth: "The hour of battle has struck. The enemy surrounds us on all sides. We need auxiliary troops, if possible, under the command of Self-Renunciation, who has seen active service in previous campaigns against Error." On receipt of this important despatch, Truth summons his most trusted officers. Humility is to fight against I-Come-First, Holy Obedience against Cocksure's uproarious host, and Charity against Bigotry. Renunciation is made commander-in-chief.

Truth and his forces gain a complete victory, and march on Benares. Error is mortally wounded. Mâya, or cosmic illusion, has called him into this transitory existence. Being on the point of death, Error sends the talisman Mâya back to his grandfather Infinite.

Salvation-by-works is the wife of Individual Consciousness. When she learns that her darling son Error is dead, the shock kills her. Prince Vedânta speaks comfort to the bereaved husband, and tells him that all individual grief is idle and unreal. Renunciation, the victorious warrior-saint, is then received in audience by Individual Consciousness, who bears up bravely in his personal affliction, and is more resigned, thanks to Vedânta's disinterested counsel. When the time of mourning is over, the jolly widower even thinks of remarriage. The bride-elect is his deceased wife's sister, Lady Salvation-by-faith. Hers is the golden faith which ever distrusts itself, and flows out in constant deeds of charity.

Peace-of-heart, vicegerent of Infinite, now enters the mansions of the King of kings, and finds Science in the arms of Religion. By their side plays young Vedânta, radiant and beautiful, his face aglow with selfless love, his beaming eyes subdued by wisdom's light.

After Error's decease, Truth becomes sole regent of the universe. Bliss and Intelligence support him in the Divine government of earth.[1]

[1] Buddha means "awakened", i.e., no longer dreaming that

16. Prahasans

Laughable pieces such as *The Taming of the Shrew* or *The School for Scandal* are called prahasans in India. They are skits on social follies, brimful with vulgar wit and catchy puns. Like our curtain-raiser, a prahasan has one act only. DHÛRTA SAMÂGAM, or ROGUES IN COUNCIL, is the title of a spicy comedietta belonging to the fifteenth century. We subjoin a brief survey of the plot.

Dame Ananga reigns supreme in the hearts of two religious degenerates, whose debased yoga serves as a convenient cloak for chambering and jugglery. On their daily round of alms-begging, the two meet in Ananga's house. The younger mendicant, in a fit of jealousy, kicks his courting rival, who swears at him.

visible things are real. His *prabodha* (awakening, illumination) took place under the bo-tree, or Tree of Knowledge.

Calderon, in one of his metaphysical plays, compares the dense life of the senses to a dream which precedes the slumbering soul's awakening to spiritual consciousness. The risen soul, no longer clinging to the things of sense, no more in touch with earth's semblances and shadows, tastes the sweet realities of Life in God. Another play by the illustrious Spaniard is based on Daniel, Chapter V, and introduces Idolatry, Reason, and Divine Judgment among the dramatis personæ.

The quarrel waxes hot, and Ananga interferes at last. At her request the disputants agree to have their sordid difference adjusted by Asajjâti. That worthy is a brahmin by birth, and a lawyer by profession, his special calling being arbitration in cases of a delicate nature.[1] He is fetched in, and in his turn finds Ananga's charms irresistible. After listening quietly to the complaints on either side, Asajjâti makes a grave face, and turns up a big law-book. He then pronounces judgment. Both parties are advised to be friends again, and to leave Ananga alone in future. The fee for the legal consultation is rather stiff, but the monks can happily afford it,—fortune-telling, invocations of the dead, and interpretation of dreams being a profitable source of income just then.

When the two are gone, Mûlanâshaka, the barber, enters, and presents to fair Ananga her monthly bill for hair-dressing and nail-trimming. She coolly refers her creditor to Asajjâti. To ingratiate himself with the fascinating landlady, the

---

[1] Sprung from the lineage (jâti) of sophistry (asat), is the significant meaning of Asajjâti's name.

stingy jurist pays, though with a long face. As a favour in return he wants a shave and a shampoo. The wily barber feels tempted by the gold in Asajjâti's purse, and means to fleece him. He quietly asks Ananga for some packthread, and after soaping his client's face most liberally, ties the lawyer's hands and feet deftly to the heavy chair on which he sits. With the dainty skill of a professional thief, Mûlanâshaka neatly picks the brahmin's pocket, and with many a smile and apology bows himself out of the room. Ananga, standing in the background, holds her sides, and shakes with fits of laughter.

The Dhûrta Samâgam was penned about the same time as the *Mandragola*, or *Magic Potion*, by Machiavel. The Italian prahasan, too, exposes the lascivious morals that prevailed in Rome prior to the apostolate of St. Philip Neri. But the brush of the Florentine statesman was capable of finer touches than that of his Hindu contemporary.[1]

[1] The soma sacrifice which gave rise to the ninth mandala of the Rig Veda is also associated with the oldest prahasans. They were boisterous farces, rough and gruff like the rumbling and grumbling of a thunderstorm. The seeds of tragedy and buffoonery, the fatal and the comic, lie embedded side by side

17. Bhânas

Bhânas or musical sketches are extremely popular in the south of India. They sometimes last from daybreak until nightfall, with long intervals every now and then. Here is a specimen of a bhâna composed by Varada.

The sole actor sits at an open window. He plays a guitar, and greets the approach-

in nature's dissolute forces. The first burlesque ever mentioned in Indian literature re-echoes the howl and growl of the warring elements, the tomfoolery of nature. "A fat nigger who deals in soma is cheated out of a milch cow, the price of his medicinal store. The outwitted blackskin is infuriated, spits and swears, and uses wild threats, but to no purpose. However, his strong language gradually tones down to feeble notes, and his remonstrances become mild and even timid. But all he gets into the bargain is a hiding with a leather thong." The whole frolic is a brahmodya or nature conundrum in a dramatic form. The soma cordial was the delight of Indo-Iranian feasters, the seal and bond of Vedic fellowship. The milky juice of the aromatic mountain herb made an ideal drink which restored and renewed the spirit of the twice-born, even as the heavenly soma which is jealously guarded by black monster-clouds revives the thirsty vegetation. The parched earth cries out for the delicious mead, but the "liquor of the gods" (IX, 109^{15}) flows scantily, until the thunderbolt strikes the soma-hoarding miser. Like floods of milk, the silvery showers then stream from the full udder of the rain-cow; the threatening cloud-giant has to give up the fragrant ambrosia. The theatre of war up in the sky supplied the earliest Indian stage with plenty of raw material for the rude charades which were acted in that primitive and superstitious age.

ing dawn. The stillness of the sleeping city and the slowly awakening traffic in the street suggest the next item in the musical programme. A stylishly dressed woman then passes in her carriage. This trifling incident gives rise to some couplets on the fair sex in general, and on married life in particular. A variety of persons are taken off with considerable humour. The comedian next observes a large crowd gathering round a snake charmer. All at once he notices a friend over the way, and accosts him in a snatch of song. An appointment is made to meet at some popular café in the evening. Thus the artist goes on in a rambling fashion, watching and describing, chanting and responding, dropping one subject and taking up another, until the full moon is seen rising in a cloudless sky.[1]

[1] The earliest specimens of bhânas in Sanskrit literature are monologues of a ruined gambler (Rig Veda, X, 34) and of drunken Indra (X, 119). The tenth mandala also contains some prahasans, which were perhaps enacted in seasons of revelry such as preceded the long and dreary sacrifices, even as King Carnival performs his mad pranks just before the solemn season of Lent. The mimicry of a chariot race in which a buxom dame, driving a wretched ox-cart, wins the prize, is the delightful theme of a humorous sanvâda (X, 102).

18. Yâtras

The founder of Islam had a puritanical aversion to story-tellers and stage-actors. When the Mohammedans became rulers of India, they followed in the Prophet's footsteps, and abolished every music hall and playhouse. But coercion is bound to evoke reaction; that is a universal law which holds good at home and in school, in politics and religion, in society and on the stage. In spite of the Moslem precepts, dramatic activity was once more in full swing towards the end of the fourteenth century, more particularly in Nepal and Tirhut. But the literary quality of this aftercrop of Indian plays is far below the high level which was attained in Ujain and Kanouj during the classical ages of Kâlidâsa and Bhavabhûti. The revival in Bengal was religious as well as dramatic; the fermentation worked silently, but was powerful enough to infuse new life into the forsaken temples and antiquated theatres of reawakened India.

An impersonal God is all very well for subtle thinkers who can reason clearly, but

the great masses in every age and clime
need a personal Saviour who has become
man in order that fallen mankind, uplifted
by His perfect example, may draw nearer
to God. Vedântists define personal and
impersonal as the revealed and hidden side
of God, and affirm that the Deity, despite
the twofold aspect, is hypostatically one.
Like Platonists and Christians they hold
that the eternal "substance" beneath the
troubled sea of transient appearances is beyond the ken of reason, but, in its infinite
goodness taking compassion on the world,
is made manifest to the believer's vision.
When Hindu philosophy had overthrown
the Vedic pantheon, and established Brahma (the Infinite) in the vacated place of
divine manifestations, the people of India,
with a healthy religious instinct, reverted
to the worship of Râma and Krishna, whom
they regarded as His visible incarnations.
Brahma, the unqualified Deity, they could
not understand, but Krishna they believed
to be the ideal son of God. Him they
could love and adore and imitate, after
endowing him with the noblest and best
of human qualities. Krishna became the
favourite avatâr of the people, and magni-

ficent pagodas were built in his honour
along the Orissa coast. About three hundred miles south-west of Calcutta, at Jug-
gernaut, a celebrated Krishna temple was
raised as early as the twelfth century. The
Krishnaist cult, being bright and artistic,
was admirably fitted to invigorate the effete
Hindu theatre. Sacred operas were frequently produced in connection with the
religious yâtras or processions of the
Krishnaists. In a later age these musical
dramas came to be called yâtras, even after
they were detached from the temple pre-
cincts, and associated with the secular
stage. Yâtras are no longer composed in
Sanskrit or Shauraseni, but chiefly in
Bengali. The regeneration of the Indian
theatre is mainly due to these refined and
often original plays. For their present
popularity the yâtras are largely indebted
to Krishna-Kamal, pastor of the Vishnu
congregation at Dacca, north-east of Calcutta.[1]

[1] Even the Vedic age knew yâtras—a venerable heirloom of
Aryan antiquity. The gods of the Rig Veda were hymned
in choral processions. Some of the sanvâda-hymns re-echo
the rude mirth of the primitive yâtra-dances. But the alleged
affinity between Sanskrit *rig* (praise) and German *reigen* (choral
dance) is altogether uncertain, although both words point to a

Bengal has always been the stronghold of Krishnaist literature, and the starting-point for new religious movements. It was here that Jayadev wrote his beautiful Gîta Govinda. Hosts of Krishnaist poets and philosophers flourished in Bengal. It was in Bengal that Buddha preached the brotherhood of all men, irrespective of caste and colour, that Chaitanya reformed native society, and that Râmakrishna encouraged his spiritual sons to go on a

common Indo-European root expressive of gleam and gladness.

The Anglo-Saxons, too, celebrated the awakening of spring with solemn yâtras around the merry maypole. They sang the praises of gay Flora and her mother Earth, with carol and response, in truly dramatic fashion. On classical soil, morris dancers carried phallus images, the wanton emblem of procreative force, in holiday processions. Such public exhibitions, which Shivaists and Tantrists even now include in their temple services, would outrage our moral sense, but merely suggested the fruitful womb of nature to her ancient votaries. However, the pagan mysteries were bound to degrade into obscene rites and wild orgies. The early Church, not choosing to break with the popular usages and hallowed superstitions of the Gentiles, wisely grafted on to the world-old festival of spring the holier Easter rejoicings. Christ is risen at the very season when nature, clad in festive garb, rises from her long winter sleep. The depraved phallic worship had to make room for the sweet Passion plays. Hoary with the Christian traditions of more than a thousand years, they are still enacted by the peasantry at Oberammergau, and in other villages of Bavaria and the Tyrol. Religious processions gave rise to the beginnings of dramatic literature both in India and Europe.

mission to America and England, where they have boldly attempted to reconcile Christian Revelation and modern science on the deep foundation of Vedânta.

19. A Bengal Revivalist

Chaitanya was born in Nadia, towards the end of the fifteenth century. He combined, in a high degree, practical sense and moral courage. Chaitanya was a powerful preacher adorned with all the winning graces of a saint. Pratâpa, Vassal-King of Bengal, had the Reformer's sermons collected. It is possible that Chaitanya also wrote some yâtras; anyhow, he encouraged the religious melodrama on the Bengal stage, and his followers contributed plays to the Krishnaist theatre. Most prominent among them are Rûpa-Goswâmi, well known as a poet and statesman, and Karnapur, who dramatized Chaitanya's life. The piece bears the title CHAITANYA CHANDRODAY, i.e. the Rise of Chaitanya's Luminary, and is regarded by literary critics as the finest Krishnaist play.

20. Chaitanya Chandroday

Chaitanya is on the village green. His mother, Sachi, pays him homage, and a happy group of peasant girls sing praises to the latest incarnation of Krishna.

In the second act, Chaitanya's favourite disciples, Bhakti and Adwaita, converse on the nature of faith. Both walk together to the house of Chaitanya's uncle, where a dramatic performance of the Gîta Govinda is to be given.

Chaitanya intimates his intention to become a sannyâsi.[1] He parts from his native place, and Ganga weeps that the saint has left her shores. The tears of the river goddess mingle freely with those of Father Ocean, to whom she narrates the touching farewell scenes which she has witnessed.

Pilgrims arrive from the Carnatic coast, and from the banks of the river Godavery. They cannot tell enough of the marvellous conversions which the saint has wrought.

---

[1] A saint who has broken every link in the chain of natural affection. Complete self-surrender deepens his God-consciousness (=chaitanya) and interior peace.

Chaitanya returns from his missionary tour. King Pratâpa and his Prime Minister, Rûpa-Goswâmi, beg to be accepted among his followers.[1]

21. Universal Religion

Our task is nearly finished. We have traced the hidden sources of the Indian theatre, and have rapidly surveyed its variegated course through scenery most enchanting. We lost sight of the dried-up current amidst shallow sands and in the mudbanks of frivolity. We watched the last efforts of the decadent drama to

[1] Bhakti and Adwaita are symbolical names. The former means devotion to a Supreme Personality—the yearning for the love and pardon of an avatâr. The test of bhakti is utter self-abasement, but fearless and never servile. A-dwaita or non-dualism teaches that a self-effaced (nirvâna) soul and the eternal spring of all created life are not dual, i.e. separate, but one in essence. A dull and vacant frame of mind is the very opposite to the nirvâna state, since a spiritual combatant must ever watch and distrust himself, ere he can hope to slay the hundred-headed serpent of selfishness and sluggishness, and, with the knife of gnâna, tear up the deep-rooted weeds of dwaita in the garden of his soul. As Christians believe that original sin is inherited, and that baptism removes the moral stain, so dwaita, in the eyes of Adwaitists, is inbred in every man until the Adwaita philosophy (Vedânta) removes mâya, i.e. the "great illusion".

The classical exposition of bhakti is given in the Bhagavad Gîta; of adwaita in the Great Jungle Upanishad.

emerge, purified, from the dreary quag-
mire, and to enlist in the cause of national,
and, as we shall see presently, of universal
religion.

(a) Two Great Mogul Emperors

Timur Khan and his savage hordes
captured Delhi about the year 1400, but
the Mogul Empire did not gain a firm
hold on India until the beginning of the
sixteenth century, when Babar, sixth in
descent from Timur, sat on the peacock
throne. Babar was daring in the field,
and prudent in council. He fought many
victorious battles during his short-lived
reign. After a day's hard fighting, the
great Kaiser would retire to the quiet of
his tent and compose Persian poetry, the
elegance and propriety of which have been
much admired. Nanak, who lived in his
reign, conceived the lofty idea of blending
Islam with Hinduism. He felt that the
spiritual kernel in both religions is the
same, however much the historical husk
and the overgrowth of dogma may vary.
Chaitanya, in his extensive travels, possibly made the personal acquaintance of

Nanak, and may even have influenced his teaching. The new faith was to do away with Hindu idolatry and Moslem fanaticism, but to retain what was acceptable to both sides and offensive to neither. The movement spread among the Punjab aristocracy, and the nobles who gathered round Nanak called themselves his sikhs or disciples. The Sikhs are a splendid race of soldiers, as might be expected of the martial Rajputs from whose ranks they chiefly issued. The scriptures of the Sikhs are monotheistic, and their moral stamina and religious zeal recall some of the finest Hebrew types depicted in the Old Testament, whilst in courage and physique the sons of Nanak are superior to the children of Israel.

Akbar, a grandson of Babar, ruled over Hindustan in the sixteenth century. Just as Brahmins and Buddhists had served King Harsha with equal loyalty, so Hindus and Moslems forgot their acrimony and rivalry in a common feeling of devotion to Akbar. Under that best of Indian emperors, every religion, Christianity included, enjoyed full liberty and equal privileges. Akbar was a strict Mus-

sulman himself, but some of the highest
government posts were filled by Hindu
officials. He had the New Testament
translated from Greek into Persian, and
ordered an Allah Upanishad to be written.
Under his auspices, weekly meetings were
convened in the royal palace to set forth
doctrinal differences fearlessly, and give
the rival arguments an impartial hearing.
There is but One True God, exclaims a
Vedic seer, though they whom He inspires
call Him by many names.[1] He is the
Soul of our souls, the Self of ourselves,
and as long as we love Him and trust in
Him with the simple faith of children, it
matters little whether His name be Allah
or Jehovah, the Infinite and Absolute, or
Our Father and Creator. Names are but
fumes of incense after all. The Emperor
Akbar made the same bold and bright
declaration of faith.

"O God! in every temple and in every
tongue I hear the people praise Thee.
Every religion says, Thou art Adwaita—
One without a second. Islam and polytheism feel after Thee. Whether I frequent Mosque or Pagoda, Thee I search

---

[1] Ekam sat viprâh bahudhâ vadanti (Rig Veda I, 164).

in every sanctuary. Thy elect are neither orthodox nor heterodox, but stand behind the screen of Thy veiled Truth, as lotuses and roses feed on the selfsame mother-soil."

> "Shall the rose
> Cry to the lotus: no flower thou? the palm
> Call to the cypress: I alone am fair?
> The mango spurn the melon at his foot?"[1]

But however broad and tolerant the views of Akbar were, his Moslem subjects could not leave the infidels alone. The same violent fanaticism which has broken out, over and over again, in Bulgarian atrocities and Armenian massacres, found vent, at an earlier age, in the cruel persecution of the Hindus which began soon after Akbar's death.

(b) The Sikhs

The Sikhs were quite willing to mediate between the two races and religions, but fared worst. While the mild natives of Oudh and Bengal suffered terribly from Mohammedan cruelties, and offered but little resistance, the high-minded Sikhs

---

[1] Quoted from Tennyson.

were Rajputs (which means Sons of
Kings), and had inherited the warlike
propensities shown by their Aryan sires
thousands of years ago; the early Vedic
colonists doggedly wrested the Punjab
from the savage aborigines by endless
guerrilla wars.   Nanak's faith was vigor-
ously defended with the sword, and the
Sikhs became the bitterest enemies of the
Mogul Empire.

The Hindu character, whatever its de-
fects may be, is singularly devoid of
bigotry and fanaticism, which darken so
many pages of Mohammedan history.
Nevertheless we must bear in mind that,
during the Moslem age, secret societies
were at work in the Punjab, and endeavoured surreptitiously to overthrow the
ruling power.   The conspirators held their
seditious conventicles under the guise of
religious meetings, and it was an act of
self-protection on the part of the Government if they punished the offenders, and
suppressed Hinduism as a hotbed of re-
volutionary plots.[1]   No doubt, excessive

---

[1] Just as England and Germany have been compelled at times
to use armed force in order to put down Fenian aspirations
or Polish nationalism.

zeal often led to massacres both in medieval India and Europe.   But the Mogul
Throne did not always sanction, and the
Christian Church had often to restrain, the
fanatical outbreaks of an enraged populace, despite the oft-repeated reproach that,
in the Middle Ages, by ecclesiastical command, many a noble soul that dared em-
bark on a perilous sea of adverse currents

"perished at the stake
For tenets he would not forsake".

In the beginning of the eighteenth century, Râja Guru Govinda was the leading
chieftain of the Sikh clans.[1]   Military ambition and religious conviction urged him
on to break down all prejudice of caste,
and he freely invited vaishyas and shûdras
to join his standard against the hated
oppressor.   But although the Sikhs fought
with the fierceness of tigers and the courage of lions,[2] they were utterly routed by
the Imperialist forces.   Those who escaped

[1] Guru and Sikh (Master and Disciple) are chips of the old
Vedic phraseology.   "Shepherd, Teacher, King" is the literal
rendering, if we reverse the order of words, of Râja Guru
Govinda.

[2] They were actually called singhs or lions, and Singh is
still a patronymic of many Sikh and Rajput families.

from the battlefield were hunted like wild beasts from one stronghold to another. No more was heard of them for another generation. But about 1740, at that unhappy period when the Jacobites rose for the doomed cause of the exiled Stuart family, the Sikhs likewise rallied, and once more issued from their mountain fastnesses that they might overthrow the Mogul dynasty. The insurgents met with varying successes. Being masters of Lahore at one time, they were repulsed, on another occasion, with a loss of a hundred thousand men. Although the Sikhs had a National Council, they never became a nation, but were always split up into numbers of petty free-states, which were disaffected and disunited because of the constant jealousies and dissensions among their chieftains.[1]

Their most powerful chief was Ranjit

[1] It was in 1745 that the Celtic clans of Scotland gave active support to Charles Edward the Pretender in his gallant but hopeless attempt to regain the throne of England, and re-establish the Catholic faith. Gael and Sikh, in their tribal pride, military valour, and extravagant notions of honour, strongly resemble each other. Never-ending domestic feuds and clannish obstinacy enfeebled the brave Punjab men quite as much as the Scotch Highlanders, and greatly facilitated the ultimate subjection of both races to British rule.

Singh.   He ruled in the Punjab about
1800; the seat of his government was
Lahore.   Other Sikh republics lay scattered between the Sutlej and Jumna; all
of which repudiated Ranjit's claim to over-
lord them.   Prince Ranjit then appealed
to the English, and Lord Metcalfe con-
cluded a treaty of friendship with the State
of Lahore.   The debatable land between
the two rivers was placed under British
protection, and nowadays the various Sikh
clans form native states with a British
resident.

(c) Church Universal

The idea of a universal church, which is
discussed in American magazines as the
latest novelty in religion, has engaged the
Hindu mind for many centuries.   In the
Mohammedan era, Hinduism was ready
for amalgamation with Islam, and under
English rule it is equally prepared to join
forces with Christianity.   Rammohun Roy,
who died in Bristol about 1830, was a
sound Vedic and Biblical scholar.   After
many years of close and critical study he
felt convinced that the teachings of Jesus,
in their substance, coincide with the tenets

of Vedânta.   It was the noble ideal of this
great and good man to bring the upper
classes of England and India nearer in
fellow-feeling on the basis of their common
faith.   But while Rammohun Roy was
more of a scholar and a saint, Keshub
Chunder Sen, a devoted friend of Râmakrishna, had a thoroughly practical turn
of mind.   He took up Rammohun's work,
and even attempted the fusion of all three
religions into what he called the New Dis-
pensation.   Like Chaitanya he made use
of the stage for popularizing his religious
views.   It was by his encouragement that
the dramatist Trailokya wrote the NAVA
VRINDÂVAN.[1]   Keshub himself acted the
Yogi in the play, and carried a cosmopolitan banner with a curiously embroi-
dered design.   Cross and Crescent were
lovingly interlaced with Buddhist and
Hinduist emblems.   A dove representing
the Holy Ghost seemed to succumb to
the hard blows of human reason, but

[1] Zealous Krishnaists have the same reverence for Vrindâvan Forest, the scene of the youthful follies of their shepherd-
god, as devout Christians, with a far better right, have for the
Holy City.   In some respects, the Nava (i.e. New) Vrindâvan
corresponds to the New Jerusalem depicted in the Book of
Revelation, chapter xxi.   The resemblance is perhaps due
to Christian influences.

the heaven - descended bird reascended
triumphantly, bearing around his neck the
inscription : "Long live the New Dis-
pensation!"

Keshub Sen had not the slightest intention of attacking or belittling the Christian
conception of the Holy Ghost.   On the
contrary, he wished to intimate that the
secular spirit of the age ever resents the
Holy Mysteries, which the human mind,
limited as it is to the cognition of phenomena, can only receive under the humble
veil of appearances.

Since Sanskrit began to be taught by
the side of Greek in the Universities of the
West, Christendom has grown familiar with
Indian beliefs.   Comparative Theology is
studied, more and more, in ecclesiastical
seminaries.   Many theologians hold that
Divine Providence has designed and disclosed every religion, even the crudest and
lowest, until, in the fulness of time, the
Word was made flesh, and dwelt among
us.   As in a French, Burmese, and Turkish
brain, provided there is a similar mental
temperament, the identical thoughts are at
work, however much the language may
differ in which they are expressed—such

is the argument used—so the same spirit
of Truth wrestles in the souls of Christians,
Buddhists, and Moslems, seeking expression in various formulas of faith.

The keynote of all religion is man's
sacrifice to God, and God's to man.   The
Deity ever responds to self-sacrifice, and
showers graces on prayerful souls.   God's
perfect sacrifice, the Incarnation, could
not take place until the human race had
evolved a type of man ready to tread the
narrow path marked out by Christ, and
to follow in His footsteps patiently, willing to bear each cross that comes, even
as the Master bore His to Calvary.

If we interpret the signs of the time
rightly, this restless and fermenting age
yearns for a Catholicism broad enough to
include all the world's religious aspirations
both great and small.   This yearning has
found an eloquent expression in the Parlia-
ment of Religions held at Chicago in 1893,
the year of the World's Fair.   There could
be seen followers of Christ and Buddha
side by side with believers in Zoroaster
and Laotse.   Synagogue and Mosque
sent distinguished delegates.   Râmaists
and Tantrists were present.   It was a

thoroughly representative gathering of the
principal religions of the world.   Each
exponent discussed the verities and virtues
of his respective faith in an amicable spirit,
free from all bitterness and needless controversy.   "Christian faith and morals",
was the bold declaration of a learned sannyâsi, "have happily absorbed the philo-
sophies of Plato and Aristotle, the two
loftiest peaks of pagan wisdom in the
West.   May God raise another Angelic
Doctor to merge holy Vedânta, the sub-
limest system of Eastern speculation, with
even farther-reaching results, into Christian
Revelation."

To which we add: And may it be the
privilege of the twentieth century to foster
that sweet spirit of tolerance and tenderness, and thus advance the progress of
God's Universal Church!

APPENDIX

Aryan Roots[1]

After parting with their Indo-Iranian
kinsmen, the Aryan main stock passed
through a common period of agriculture,
probably in the south-west of Russia.
From there the Teutonic tribes seem to
have trekked through Galicia and Poland,
and entered the lowlands of Germany,
whilst the classical and Celtic clans jour-
neyed together along the Danube. Subsequently the Celts, left to themselves, occu-

---

[1] In a work on the Greek Theatre, it would be quite un-
necessary to explain the meanings of "drama" and "chorus",
or "epic" and "rhapsody", because classical antiquity has
bequeathed all these terms to us. But modern culture has
little or no connection with the ideals of ancient India. It
is hoped that the various derivations scattered throughout
these pages, and often relating to words that have no direct
bearing on the stage, will be found helpful by the general
reader. The selected examples which are traced back to
Aryan roots all occur in the present volume or in the *Short
History*.

pied the Central Rhinelands. About B.C.
2000 or 1500, when bronze came to be used
by the side of polished stone, the European
Aryans were seated in their oldest historic
settlements.

The Germans call themselves Dutch
(*deutsch*), and give to both nations as well as
to their English and Scandinavian cousins
the common title German (*germanisch*),
which, therefore, means the same as Teutonic does in England. The Teutons, together with the Celts, whom they have
more or less absorbed, form the western-
most branch of the Aryan family of speech.
German scholars prefer the name *Indo-
German* to *Aryan*, which suggests to them
Indo-Iranian only. Persian, they say, is a
West-Aryan tongue, and the Hindu vernaculars are East-Aryan. Indo-European
seems a happier expression than Indo-
German, because Sanskrit, Greek, and
Latin, the languages of Iran and Erin,
Teutonic and Slavonic, were distributed
from India to Europe since prehistoric
times. The word Aryan recommends itself
by its brevity, and, by long-continued
usage, is more familiar to Englishmen than
Indo-European or Indo-German. We

subjoin a table of the various terms, with
their German equivalents.

England.		Germany.
Teutonic	=	German.
German	=	Dutch.
Dutch	=	Hollandish.
East-Aryan	=	Aryan.
Aryan	=	Indo-German.

West-Aryan speech comprises Teutonic and
Romance, Gaelic and Welsh, the Balkan
tongues and Russian.

The Aryan race is split up into a variety
of languages and dialects, but all Aryan
tongues have a common stock of root-
words and, consequently, of radical ideas.
Daylight (Latin dies) and the bright sky
(Sanskrit div or diu),[1] as well as Ju-piter
(Father Sky), are cognate notions flowering
on the same tree of thought. *Ved*a refers
to the heavenly *vi*sion which pure-souled
seers "see" (√ vid),[2] and shruti is revealed
truth to which inspired hearers "listen"
(√ shru).   A twin verb of the former root
is Latin vid-ere; of the latter, Anglo-Saxon
hly-stan, our li-sten.[3]   √ vish (move in,

---

[1] Pronounce "dew".

[2] √ indicates a root-word.

[3] As regards the change from shru to hly, see *Short History*,
chapter viii, footnote to shruti.

settle) and √ kri (make, do) have ramified over the whole area of Indo - European speech. Vaishya (settler, burgher), Latin vicus (settlement, borough), whence village is derived, and English place-names such as Alnwick, a Northumbrian village on the romantic Aln banks, have all sprung from vish. Creator, karma and prakriti, Prâkrit and Sanskrit itself, are rooted in the mental soil of kri.[1]

Throughout the realm of nature, light, sound, and motion are conjoint forces. Where one is manifest, the others are also present. The Âryas, gifted children of nature as they were, reflected, even in their first attempts of speech, the bright image of their mother. Word never passed the lips of Vedic rishi or Persian mage, Greek rhapsodist or Northern saga-teller, Roman or British orator, which cannot be reduced to a root expressive of the tripartite sense of light (div) or vision (vid), sound or hearing (shru), and movement (vish) or activity (kri). At first the roots were few,

---

[1] Creator = Maker. Karma = our past doings; habits formed; character built up. Prakriti = procreation, nature. Prâkrit = "natural" speech; not cultivated like Sanskrit, but growing wild as the flowers in the field. Sanskrit = the perfect creation and full expression of the Indian mind.

each having threefold force, but as the
mind branched out, they multiplied and
retained one sense only, which became a
feeder of profoundest thought—the source
of Aryan religion and philosophy.[1] Karma
and dharma, character and the sense of
duty, really the fruits of "action" and the
moral "hold", are evolved from kri and
dhar.   The germ-idea of dharma is dhar,
that is, to hold or bind.   Limitation inherent
in finite matter is a more scientific phrase,
but conveys no more than dharma.   The
vocable displays a wealth of ethical meaning.   "Form" and "custom" have a firm
hold on society; all "law" is binding;
"re-lig-ion", too, enjoins many an ob-lig-
ation; "environment" and "idiosyncrasy"
hold the individual with an iron grip—all
this and more is involved in dharma.   There
is an Indian saying that this life's karma
shapes dharma in the next; that is to say,
the use which a man makes of his present
opportunities determines his future circum-
stance.

*Brah*ma and pra*kri*ti—God and nature

---

[1] "Go", the Sanskrit for cow, has actually retained the three
meanings: (1) shining "stars", (2) lowing "kine", (3) the
hurled "thunderbolt", the winged "arrow".

—have sprung from the same cluster of roots (brih and kri). It is noteworthy that the supreme god of the brahmins was originally not conceived as motionless and passive, but as *cre*ative (kri), i.e. active. The definition of Brahma as expansion (brih) of the prayerful heart is a priestly afterthought, far too subtle and scholastic to have a place in primitive culture. The simpler notion of a nature spirit, or, as we should say, of cosmic energy "breaking forth" (brih), as star and flower, wood and stream, and as the cloud-hid "mountains" (ge*birg*e in German), is more in harmony with the naïve sentiments of a vigorous and youthful race. Only the trained linguist or the poet's finer fancy can discern in the clipped coinage of our polished tongues the flash and rush and roar of the wild elements, and the native charm of meadowland and forest, distilled in triple essence.

List of Dates[1]

B.C.

2000–1500	The Indo-Europeans in their oldest historic settlements.
6th – –	Rise of Buddhism.
4th – –	Pânini.
327 – –	Alexander invades India.
*303 – –	Chandragupta defeats Seleucus.
3rd – –	Ashoka — Buddhism introduced in Ceylon.
2nd – –	Pushpamitra and Agnimitra.
1st – –	Pâli Canon committed to writing.

A.D.

5th & 6th	Decline of Magadha and of Indian Buddhism — Rise of the Gupta dynasty and of Hinduism—Kâlidâsa.
6th & 7th	Many Hindu Temples built in Orissa — Sanskrit still in official use — "The Toy Cart".
7th – –	Harsha — Bâna — Dandin — I-Tsing visits India.
*700 – –	Bhavabhûti.

[1] Dates marked * are approximate, and "—th" indicates the century.

9th -	-	Adwaita systematized—Bhatta Nârâyan—Shivaswâmi.
10th -	-	Râjashekhar.
*1000 -	-	Mahmud of Ghazni invades India.
11th -	-	Rajputs, rulers of India—The Brihat Katha twice recast in Sanskrit — Dâmodar.
12th -	-	"Gîta Govinda"—"Prabodha Chandroday"— perhaps "Mudra - Râkshasa".
13th -	-	Chenghiz Khan—Moslems, rulers of India.
*1400 -	-	Timur captures Delhi.
15th -	-	"Rogues in Council."
16th -	-	Babar and Akbar — Chaitanya and Nanak.
17th -	-	Death of Tulsi Das—Râmabhadra.
18th -	-	Râja Guru Govinda.
*1800 -	-	Ranjit Singh.
19th -	-	Keshub Sen and Trailokya — Comparative Philology centres in Sanskrit and Phonetics.
1893 -	-	"Parliament of Religions" at Chicago.
20th -	-	Philological Research devoted, more and more, to Semantics and Indo-European Civilization.[1]

[1] As far back as the 18th century scholars felt the need of a semantic vocabulary, dealing with European terms of culture. "There is room for a very interesting work which should lay open the connection between the languages and manners of nations" (Gibbon, *Decline*, Chapter I).

Words Explained

1. ENGLISH

brother, 72.
create, 198.
heathen, 15.
morris, 160.

pelican, 138.
populous, 35.
punch, 155.

religion, 199.
rook, 117.
village, 198.

2. GERMAN

gebirge, 200 | reigen, 178–9.

3. GREEK AND LATIN

gnosis, 11. | polis, 35. | vicus, 198.

4. INDIAN

amrita (ambrosia), 125.
bhat (actor), 22, 72.
brahmacharya (chastity), 129.
brahmodya (riddle), 116.
dharma (duty), 199.
gnâna, 11.
karma, 198.
Marathi, 29.
nâgari, 15.
panchâli (puppet), 154–5.
prakriti (nature), 198.

pur (town), 35.
rath (chariot), 117.
rig, 19, 178–9.
Sanskrit, 198.
shakunta, 63.
shruti (revealed, i.e. Veda), 197.
sûtradhâra (stage manager), 155.
vaishya (settler), 198.
vânar (monkey), 139.
Veda, 197.

5. NAMES AND PLACES

Index